C000295148

# My Autobiography

## Mansfield Born & Bred

To Michelle -
With love
from
Ian White

**My Autobiography – Mansfield Born & Bred**

Copyright © Mary White 2016 All Rights Reserved

The rights of Mary White to be identified as the author of this work have been asserted in accordance with the Copyright, Designs and Patents Act 1988

All rights reserved. No part may be reproduced, adapted, stored in a retrieval system or transmitted by any means, electronic, mechanical, photocopying, or otherwise without the prior written permission of the author or publisher.

Spiderwize
Remus House
Coltsfoot Drive
Woodston
Peterborough
PE2 9BF

www.spiderwize.com

A CIP catalogue record for this book is available from the British Library.

The views expressed in this work are solely those of the author and do not necessarily reflect the views of the publisher, and the publisher hereby disclaims any responsibility for them.

Royalties will go to Framework for
all the wonderful work they do
www.frameworkha.org

# MANSFIELD
# BORN & BRED

*My Autobiography*

MARY WHITE

I dedicate this autobiography
to the people of Mansfield
and to those who worked with me
to create better services
for the homeless and for rejected young people
in need of family care

And to Janet Feery
who started me on that road

# INTRODUCTION

This is the story of my life, from birth in 1939 to the present day, 2016. I feel that I have lived an extraordinary life. Throughout I have met some of the most amazing, caring people and some very special professionals who have made a profound difference to the lives of some of the most vulnerable children and young people in the Mansfield, Ashfield and Nottingham areas, proving that many people do care. I remember when factories, cotton mills and mines produced thriving communities. How, after the war, all the people stood together united, when neighbours helped each other, when coal mining was our largest industry and our market trading the best; farmers traded at the cattle markets and made a good living, working hard to produce fresh organic food without additives; families had to pull together to survive and poor families were means tested to get help from the benefits system. I saw all the changes up to leaving school and right through my teens; how things changed for the better going into the 60s.

I had been brought up to work. I went through rough patches and somehow I always bounced back and became stronger. What I couldn't understand was that things were changing so quickly and we didn't see it coming. Jobs and industries were on a downhill slope and by the mid 60s we had a new problem: the plight of the homeless. Throughout the 70s and 80s it was not just homeless young people, it was homelessness in general: families, single homeless, women and children fleeing violence, and the elderly as well.

In 1957, when I was working for the Mansfield District Traction Company, I met a conductor who became my friend: Muriel Janet May Feery. When we were on a split shift and on a break we would go to the canteen for a game of cards. I lost contact with Janet at the end of 1959 when I joined the army. I met up with her again when I came home to care for my mother and I went back on the buses. Janet was homeless by then and I found out that she was having to sleep rough at the bus depot. I took Janet home to live with us until she could find accommodation for her young son, Andrew, and herself. Then we lost touch again after I got married in 1962. It was Janet who came to my rescue in 1966 when I was made homeless with my two young children, Paul and Lynn. Janet took us off the streets and gave us a home. Janet also gave me a job and I worked with her to help pay towards our board and keep. She taught me everything about running a home for the homeless. When she took ill she asked me to make her two promises: that I would bring up her son Andrew and that I would continue to look after the home and keep fighting for the plight of homeless.

It was after losing Janet - who was only 45 - that I realised my life had been planned out for me. I kept both of those promises. The people mentioned in my book are some of those who helped me to fight for the homeless hostels in Mansfield, and for 25 years we had the best homeless hostels in the country. Not only was my heart feeling for the homeless, it was feeling for youngsters from broken homes and children in care, and without the help of social workers and many professional people I would not have been able to do the work I did for Mansfield, Ashfield and the county of Nottinghamshire. Working with the homeless and vulnerable people of all kinds, as well as fostering, has given me a full life and the rewards have been in seeing them successfully move on to independence, overcoming their disadvantages. I can't count the people who went through my hands; all I know is that, without any doubt, I would do it all over again.

# CONTENTS

# CHAPTER 1

# BIRTH AND NURSERY DAYS

I was born on the 29<sup>th</sup> March, 1939, at my parents' home: 77 Newgate Lane, Mansfield, Nottinghamshire, England. I was born two months early, a premature baby weighing only two pounds one ounce. The midwife and my mum thought I was stillborn and put me at the end of the bed. Then the midwife noticed that my foot moved and realised that I was alive. They could not bath me - I was so tiny - so the nurse put me in cotton wool and olive oil to clean me. There were no incubators available for home births at this time; no one knew if I would survive. Obviously I was a little fighter, I was here and I was here to stay! I was christened Patricia Mary Crowder at St Peter's Church in the town.

I only have one memory before the age of three. My grandma had a party to celebrate my uncle Eric coming home on leave. He was in the Navy; he was my mum's youngest brother. My dad got drunk and started a fight; he got angry and left the party. He grabbed my brother Frank and me to take us home. I couldn't walk all the way, so Dad picked me up on to his shoulders and carried me home. The country was at war. The Second World War had started in September 1939, six months after I was born.

Our home consisted of a sitting room, living room and a back kitchen, two bedrooms, an attic and a cellar, with no bathroom. We had a tin bath that used to hang up outside near the back door. The toilet was at the top of the yard with newspaper cut into squares to use for toilet paper; it was freezing in winter. When we used to wake up in the morning our bedroom windows were covered in frost, leaving pictures that resembled trees and leaves. It was cold but some of the pictures on the glass looked pretty and you don't see icicles as large today!

We had chamber pots under our beds to save us going out to the toilets at night. I remember Mum making me empty them as one of my chores. Mum would tell me to empty the slops, so my brother used to torment me by renaming me "Lizzy Slop Cabbage". In the living room we had a large, black-lead fireplace with an oven on one side, a water boiler on the other, and a kettle holder that used to swing over on the fire to boil the kettle. To make our toast we used to put our bread on a toasting fork up against the fire. Mum had a dolly tub and poncher to do her washing, a rub board and a bar of carbolic soap, and a mangle we had to turn, with two rubber rollers to put the washing through to squeeze out the water. There was a copper boiler in the corner of the kitchen with a fireplace underneath to boil whites and sheets, and a flat iron that was placed near the fire till it got hot to do the ironing. Sometimes we were allowed to have a bath in the copper when Mum wasn't using it. There was a gas water boiler with a movable tap that could be swung over the sink or copper for filling with hot water.

We had no electric light; we had gas mantles, oil lamps and candles. Looking after the home was hard work for our mums in those days. We didn't have a television, just a Redifusion radio with one channel and an old wind-up record player. Everything was on ration. There was a shortage of everything but Dad kept pigs in his garden for meat. He grew all his own vegetables and had a flower bed. Every family was issued with ration books. They were poor times but people helped each other; the unity among the people was amazing.

At the age of 3, in 1942, I started nursery at Newgate Lane School. The first thing I saw was the big rocking horse. My teacher was Miss Bradbury. She took me to the cloakroom and explained that my peg had a picture of a little yellow duck above it; that was where I had to hang my coat. She also explained that my wash basin, my beaker and my smock also had a picture of a little yellow duck, and to remember they were mine to use when I was at school. There was a large Jungle Jim climbing frame, sand pit and swings on the playing out area. If I climbed to the top of the Jungle Jim I could see over the fence. Trains passed by on one side, and on the other side it looked over to the playing fields and the playground to the infants' school. It was good to look over when the infants were out at play - the noise of delight was of happy children.

The only thing I didn't like was that we were supposed to go to sleep in the afternoons. We had to sleep on little canvas beds but my mind was too active - I couldn't go to sleep. I stayed in the nursery for two years until I was five, then I moved up into the infants. I was so happy when my teacher told us she was going up with us: it meant we had another year with our nursery teacher. A new teacher, Mrs Pritchard, took her place in the old nursery. My first year in the infants' class was exciting - I was learning to count, draw, paint and to sing nursery rhymes. With the war and the shortage of certain foods we used to get a free bottle of milk at break and at lunch free orange juice, all provided by the government. We were given a tablespoon of cod-liver oil and malt: it looked a bit like treacle. I was fortunate - I liked it. To see the look on the children's faces that didn't like it; they would screw up their faces and scowl, making excuses to get out of taking it. I enjoyed my school dinners, they were free. We were not allowed to go home during the dinner breaks although I lived next door but one to the school. Mum had to collect me at home time. In between our house and the school gate was a little sweet shop run by our neighbour, Nellie Henton. She was always very busy as all the children used to go in on their way to school or when they came out of school for sweets.

The time had come when my nursery days were over. I was five now and only two years away from going up into the junior school. We were split up into two classes. I felt I was one of the lucky ones - I went into Mrs Hall's class, she was a lovely teacher. I knew her - I had been to her home, a farm on Skegby Lane, with my dad to deliver her coal. She gave me a chart with my times tables to help me with maths. It was hard, I had to memorise them and learn them that year. My writing was a nightmare, I was writing some of my letters backwards. At playtimes Mrs Hall would come outside with us to play games with the whole class: "Farmer's in his Den", "Oranges and Lemons", and "London Bridge Is Falling Down" - three of the games I will always remember.

My life at home was changing and it was affecting my school life. My mum and dad were always shouting at each other, Dad was always getting drunk at the weekends, and my brother was always blaming me for the things he did wrong. My mother always believed him. He was stealing money from her purse, stealing sweets, telling Mum he had seen me going into her purse to take the blame away from him. I didn't need to steal as my pocket money always lasted me, but Frank was spending his to buy friends. He tried to take my money. I got wise and asked my dad to save mine for me until I needed it. Frank threatened me with a carving knife; he stuck it into my side. I picked up the poker and hit him on the head with it. He had a lovely lump on his head as big as a golf ball. We had woken Dad up; he had been sleeping off his lunch time binge. Dad came running down the stairs without his trousers on, though he made sure he'd covered up his dignity. He told me to fetch his brother, Uncle Cyril, from across the road to take Frank to the hospital. Guess who got the blame. Mum was so angry with me she got the copper stick out. I ran to get out of her way to give her time to calm down. I was the one that always got punished with the copper stick and it hurt, especially when Mum was really angry.

Mum was threatening to leave Dad, saying she would move in with Grandma, telling Dad I was too much like him. Dad looked at Frank and chose not to comment. I didn't want to be the cause of trouble between my mum and dad; they were already getting close to splitting up. When Dad went out Frank lied to my mum again. That was the final straw for me; I got him under the table and pulled him up by his ears, banging his head on the floor. Mum pulled me off him and threw me out into the backyard. I was so angry I threw a stone at the window in a temper and broke a pane of glass. I had to pay for it out of my pocket money.

Although I wasn't close to my mum I did love her and couldn't stand to see her hurt. She was good to me sometimes, giving me birthday parties and taking me on holidays. It was Frank who was putting a wedge between us and I began to drift away from my mum. I didn't want to stay at home when my dad wasn't there. He took me to work with him most of the time, whenever he could. During the school holidays I was always with him. At weekends we spent time at my grandmother's, playing games with our cousins. Grandad was a Methodist; he played the organ at church on Sundays. After Sunday dinner we would all go into the sitting room where the family could sit down together and sing hymns while Grandad provided the music. Once a month we would go round to other aunts and uncles; they took it in turns like on a rota, so that the whole family were together at least once a month. We played games in Grandma's sitting room, while our parents played cards or dominoes in the living room. My dad just preferred not to go, he chose to stop at home to have a drink on his own.

Back at school I had moved up to my final year. Mrs Goodwin, my teacher, knew my mum and seemed to understand how I felt. She never put any pressure on me at school. Her daughter, Judith, used to play with me in the playground and we became good friends. After school I could guarantee I would be climbing the drainpipes or getting into trouble fighting. I was a tomboy, a wildcard; I loved my freedom. My mother encouraged me to go swimming. She herself was a strong swimmer; she won the highest award for swimming, the rose bowl, when she was at school.

My mum was talented, she used to sing and play the piano. We had a piano in our sitting room. My uncle Eric came on leave and my mum put on a party for him at our house. My dad and Uncle Eric got on well together and the party was great. Mum and Uncle Eric played a duet together on the piano: it was awesome! My mum looked happy, she had a beautiful voice. That was the last time we ever saw Uncle Eric. His submarine was blown up when it ran into an enemy mine at sea. I was with my grandmother when she received the message from the Home Office to say my uncle was lost at sea. He was my grandmother's youngest son, only nineteen. I shared all her emotions: I cried for her and with her.

My grandma told me that Mum was expecting another baby sometime soon. I had noticed that Dad had tried to stop drinking and I was praying that this could last. We had won the Second World War the year before and we had celebrated Victory Day. All the streets held street parties, and flags and bunting were put up everywhere.

Things were still very much in short supply and families were still using ration books. When the street parties were organised every household donated food for the celebration; everything was homemade and tables were laden with food on every street. I never forgot Victory Day - everyone was celebrating, singing and dancing in the streets - such joy! I had never felt so much love in my life. During the war we had school lessons in the shelters when the sirens went off. I used to watch the searchlights in the sky from the top of the fire station searching for planes. We were also given rubber gas masks: every family was issued with them. After the war Dad put them all away in the attic. He had a large metal chest that he used to save the things he wanted to keep. He kept his horse brushes and the rosettes he had won with his horse, Daisy. He had entered his horse into shows for many years and in Uncle Cyril's coal yard was an old horse cart that could still be used.

I was still working, helping my dad. Mum would not let me go out to meet up with him unless I had done my chores at home. I used to get up early with Dad, clean and tidy the house and make the fire, and then I would go up to Crown Farm and wait at the weigh-bridge office for my dad to pick me up. He would give me money to go to the pit canteen for a cup of Horlicks and a Cornish pasty; he always made sure I got my breakfast. I just loved helping him to load the lorry ready for his deliveries. He was a coal merchant and haulage contractor. He would do other work after he had finished coal delivery orders - furniture removals, contract work for building firms delivering bricks, cement, sand , plaster board, etc. On Saturdays we would go to the slaughter house to collect all the cow manure. Dad would throw it on the lorry and I would be on the back of the lorry, stacking to make it safe for delivery. Doing dirty jobs didn't bother me, I got used to it. At the slaughter house Mr Mallatrat, the manager, used to bring me a fresh egg custard from the bakery department when he saw I was with my dad. I had a special pair of riding boots, real leather. Dad always made me clean them with linseed oil as it kept the leather soft and smooth. I also had a leather helmet to wear when I was working with Dad that fastened under my chin, so I can understand why I was mistaken for a boy at times.

I was brought up very strictly; my parents grew up in the Victorian era. I was brought up to have manners, to tell the truth, not to be rude to my elders, to be kind and considerate of others. Dad was always there for me, he never told me he loved me but somehow I knew he did. I only ever got a good hiding once from my dad and it was for something that I hadn't done. When I spoke to him about it he smiled and said it made up for the ones I got away with. I couldn't argue with that.

Back at school Mr Jelly, the caretaker, could never catch me. Once while he was working I borrowed his bike from the side of the nursery where he parked it against the wall. I couldn't put my leg over the cross bar so I had to ride it with my leg under it. I rode it up to the dining rooms then left it there. Mr Jelly must have thought someone had stolen it, but I only borrowed it - honest. That year was the year that I really pushed the boat out. I couldn't do anything right. Mr Jelly was intent on catching me after school, but my intention was to just go climbing on the school roofs. Then I noticed one of the cloakroom windows in the infants' school had been left open. I climbed through the window knowing Mr Jelly had gone home. Not thinking, I put the hall lights on, saw the slide and thought, "I've got it to myself". I was having a great time going up and coming down the slide; I hadn't realised that a neighbour would see the school lights on and call the police. I was coming down the slide and got a bit of a shock because the caretaker, a policeman and my mum and dad were standing in front of me. Whoops! My mum's face was like thunder. The next day I had to go to the head mistress for a telling off. Mrs Goodwin went in with me. Miss Braden, who was supposed to give me a lecture, couldn't keep a straight face. I got away with a telling off from the police. I felt I got off lightly.

That same day my mum gave birth to my baby sister. Miss Braden allowed me to go home and meet her. I looked at my baby sister and she was beautiful, I was so delighted. I went back to school to my classroom. Mrs Goodwin just smiled - I loved her, she was my favourite teacher.

That year had a bad winter - the snow was above our window ledge. Dad had to climb out of the window to clear the snow away so that we could come out of the front door. The schools had to close and everything came to a standstill. We used to go sledging on Rayner's field. One of our neighbours - a Mr Hampton Flint who was a trader in fruit and veg - lived next door to my Uncle Cyril. He painted his house white and called it the White House. Both he and his wife traded on Mansfield Market and also in the covered market. There were three entrances into the covered market, one on Queen St. The fish market was in the same place; the entrance was facing the Charter Arms. The third entrance was up by the side of the ladies' toilets, near the Swiss chalet cafe. Mr Hampton Flint used to take all us children sledging. One hard winter at the bottom of Rayner's field, near the stream, I saw a lovely gypsy caravan and went down to take a look. The gypsy lady was building a fire, and the horse was tethered. I had been told not to go near gypsies. I wrote a poem to explain my experience.

# THE GYPSY LADY

The horse was tethered, the small fire was burning
I was looking at the scene, my heart was yearning
This beautiful painted caravan was near the brook
I couldn't help myself, I needed to take a closer look

I had been warned not to talk to strangers I know
The fire looked so welcoming, glistening in the snow
Then I saw the lady, she was wrapped up very warm
My instinct told me she wouldn't do me any harm

I walked closer, she was building the fire with wood
Then I got brave - I walked right up to where she was stood
We talked for a while I soon learnt she was very kind
She invited me into her caravan, she didn't mind

Inside it was cosy, immaculate and spotlessly clean
The curtains and cushions the prettiest ever seen
The little paraffin stove she could boil the kettle on
Today she was here for me, tomorrow she'd be gone

I was made welcome, we had a chat and a cup of tea
Was it fate that we should meet or was it meant to be?
Lady in the caravan, the short time we had together,
I believe you blessed me with a caring heart for ever

It was my last week in the infants and coming up to the six week summer holidays. My memories of my life during these years are mostly happy. The first week of the holidays Mum had arranged to go up to Llandudno in Wales. We were going to spend some time with my Aunty Gladys and our cousins, Vera and Judy; they were going up on the train. Dad took us up in the lorry. Mum sat in the front with Dad and my brother and I were on the back of the lorry sitting on cushions along with the cases. You wouldn't be allowed to do that today. We stayed with Mrs Parry - Mum had worked for her in service before marrying Dad. The hotel address was 8 Trevor Street. Mr Parry was a fisherman with his own boat.

On the second day we were there my brother left the plug in the bathroom sink and the tap running. The stairs and landing were flooded, with some of the carpets floating. My brother denied leaving the tap on and put the blame on to me. Mum, as usual, believed him. My cousins knew it was Frank and said so, but it fell on deaf ears.

We went to the beach to see Mr Parry's boat and sat watching him repair his fishing nets. When it was time to go back to the hotel Frank and Vera had gone and left us and Judy was crying. We were lost and didn't know our way back to the hotel. It didn't bother me - I had seen some lovely flowers in a garden so I picked a bunch to give to my mum. Then we saw a policeman. I told him we were lost and he asked where we were staying. I told him "with Mrs Parry". He knew her and took us back to the hotel. Mum was angry with me again, saying I had no right to pick the flowers from someone's garden. Mrs Parry took the flowers and put them in a vase, saying it would be a shame to throw them away. Mrs Parry was nice to me: she bought me a big nursery rhyme book. Judy, Vera and I read the book, it had over 30 rhymes. I took the book home with me.

The most amazing thing I saw on that holiday was a hot air barrage balloon. It was shaped like a plane without the wings, and underneath was a large basket that people could get into to go up high into the sky, and then be brought back down onto the beach.

When we reached home I got into my usual routine of doing chores and going to work with Dad; afterwards I would go out to play with my friends. I had many friends: Jean my cousin lived next door, Rita lived next door but one and Glennis lived across the road. They were three of my best friends. I haven't seen much of Glennis since leaving school but Rita, Jean and I always keep in touch. We all still share our memories.

In Mansfield there were five cinemas: the Rock, Hippodrome, Grand, Granada and Empire. Dad also used to take us to the Sandhills Club on the corner of Ratcliff Rd and Broxtowe Drive to watch the old comedy films: Charlie Chaplin, Ben Turpin, Laurel and Hardy, Old Mother Riley etc, all black and white silent films shown on a white screen on the wall. We would laugh and laugh at these films, they were hilarious. We found so much to do and we didn't need lots of money to enjoy ourselves. During that year's holidays I joined the Pegasus Riding School which was owned by Jill and Sandra Charles. They lived on Newton Street and their dad was a police officer. Their aunty had a paper shop on Littleworth. I had to learn how to muck out the stables, clean and groom the horses, and how to saddle them before I was allowed to ride. Jill was a school teacher, she was very strict, I liked her. Sandra was easy-going and friendly. It was almost time for school again - I was ready to go back. My nursery and infants days were over and it was time to move on up into the juniors.

# CHAPTER 2

# MY EARLY SCHOOL DAYS

I was now 7 and started back to school in the juniors. My new teacher was Miss Dolman, she was strict but fair. She told me that I needed to memorise my 6 to 12 times tables as my maths were going to be harder. The ones I struggled with were the 8s and 9s. The maths we were given were "adds", "take aways", "times" and "divisions". Because I had learned my tables I found my maths easier and did well, so maths became my favourite subject. I could also read and spell well. We had to write with a nib pen and ink; there was an ink well on the front of our desks and I kept breaking the nib off my pen. My work book looked like a spider had walked over it. We had PT in the hall and went swimming with the school once a week. I had to learn to knit, sew and embroider. My English was rubbish: I never knew where to put my full stops or commas. I still don't know where to put them now! Geography and history I didn't like at all. Art I liked and enjoyed, RE I learnt at Sunday School. We went to Brown's Chapel on Goodacre Street. We had star cards that had to be stamped every week and we got a book as a prize if we made a full attendance.

At playtimes we played leap frog, hopscotch, skipping, ball games, marbles and snobs. We girls used to do handstands up to the wall, come down the wall with our feet and land in what we called the crab. The children caught fighting in the playground got the cane from Mr Ingham, who was our headmaster. He was far too strict. Every day there were boys and girls lining up to be punished with the cane. I saw him one day chase a boy, whacking him with the cane; the boy was running to get away from him. Children don't get the cane today. I admit I got the cane, I do believe I deserved it. I don't think it did me any harm although my hands stung and hurt. For a while that was it. Some children cried before they got the cane. I was on the cane line one morning and Mr Ingham didn't turn up. We were told to go back to our classrooms. I went back into my classroom rubbing my hands to make my friends think I'd had the cane. My teacher had not turned up and sat at her desk was Mr Ingham. What a shock! He just gave me a look and said. "Who's given you the cane Mary?" I had to think quick. I said I had been to wash my hands and I was trying to dry them. I don't think for a moment he believed me.

At home things had got bad. Mum had left Dad and gone to Grandma's. She had taken my baby sister with her and left me and Frank with Dad. She stayed at Grandma's for weeks. Dad went to ask her to come back home; he promised her he would stop his drinking. I had been

28

doing the housework but Frank did nothing to help, he really was a waste of space. Dad paid for us to have school dinners while Mum was away to make sure we had a good meal most days. At the weekend he would get us fish and chips from the fish shop and we were allowed to go down to my mum at Grandma's for our Sunday dinner. It was horrible for me, I wanted to stay at home with Dad. To hear the grown-ups calling my dad names upset me. My dad was only nasty and angry when he was drinking; most of the time he was earning the money, working hard to support the family. When he didn't have a drink my dad was the kindest person I knew. He would help anyone, give free coal to the elderly and give my mum extra money if she needed it. I used to go to bed and cry and pray to God to stop my dad from drinking.

Nothing changed. I went out to play one night after school and Rita went with me climbing on to the school roof. I still had my school shoes on - I had forgotten to change into my plimsolls. I was walking right on the top of the roof when my foot slipped on a piece of lead. I fell off the roof, rolled over the guttering and fell to the ground. I must have been unconscious for a long time. Rita had run to get help; she was frightened and didn't come back. My dad came looking for me and found me trying to drag myself across the school field. He told me when he picked me up I was limp like a rag doll. He took me to the hospital: I had broken my elbow, my leg and got concussion. I had to stay in the General Hospital. I fell unconscious and into a coma. I was in the Robin Hood Ward. After a few days I began to recover. I woke up and Mum and Dad were at the side of my bed, they were both very worried and concerned. I was in the hospital for around three weeks; all I wanted was to go home with my arm and leg in plaster. My little sister, Jacky, had started walking, so Mum had to put the safety gate on the front door to stop her getting out on to the main road. My friends came to visit me, bringing me presents to welcome me home. I could not go back to school until the plaster was taken off my leg. The school helped me by sending me some homework to save me falling behind with my education.

By the time I returned to school the summer holidays had come round again. I was moving on up into Mr Harte's class of 8 year olds. The fall had not taught me a lesson. The first chance I got I was back to climbing and back on the school roofs. I was playing out a lot more that summer. We used to play down the "avenues" as we called the road that went down to the allotments. On the left my Uncle Harold and Aunty Nellie Ancliffe had the first allotment down the lane. They kept goats and Aunty Nellie used to give us a glass of fresh goats' milk when she milked them. They had a shop on Newgate Lane just below Winston's chemists, next door to Mr Slack's cobbler's shop. The next garden was my dad's coal yard and pig sties - he used to feed the pigs and rear them until they were fat enough to be sent to the slaughter house for meat, then made into pork joints, bacon and dripping. The meat and bacon was always salted to help keep it edible and safe to consume. The bacon was hung on hooks in the cellar. Dad used to slice the bacon off as and when we needed to use it. Next to Dad's allotment was the Pegasus Riding School, owned by Gill and Sandra Charles.

Then came the railway bridge. Under the bridge the men in the area would hold a "tossing ring" where they gambled illegally for money. I often watched and saw them tossing money into the air shouting heads or tails. Whoever won picked up the money off the ground. The police would sometimes do a raid and arrest the men they caught. At the other side of the bridge both left and right were more allotments. The first on the left belonged to my dad's cousins, Frank and Fred Simms; they had stables, horses and carts with a big field for the horses. Going down to the bottom there was Mr Mellors of Arthur Street, then Dad's vegetable and flower garden and Jagger Tooth's allotment where he kept a stable, horse and cart. He was a rag and bone man who also lived on Arthur Street. Then came some waste ground leading on to Rayner's field and Sandy Lane. Opposite the waste ground was Harold Smith's allotment where he kept his horse and cart. He dealt in fruit and veg, selling them round the streets of Mansfield.

Mum started to come on to the school field with us and joined in with our games. We were playing rounders and Mum accidently got hit on the nose with the bat, causing it to bleed. When I saw the blood I felt physically sick. Mum said she was okay and didn't think her nose had been broken. We all sat down on the grass to make daisy chains then started to search for a four leaf clovers - they are supposed to be lucky. I found one but it didn't bring me any luck.

I was going to Guiler's Woods near Ravensdale with a group of my friends, Rita, Christine, Glennis and Sylvia. I was asked if I minded taking Michael along. His dad was the owner of the Brown Cow pub on Radcliffe Gate. We were playing in the stream in the woods when Michael wandered away from us - he had gone over on to the sewerage works. No one was allowed on there and we all went to fetch him back. Then, all of a sudden, Michael said, "A paddling pool!" and ran and jumped into a sewerage tank. I saw him sink then I saw his head come up. I grabbed his hair to pull him out; I needed the others to help me. I had no intention of letting go of him. I pulled him and Rita and Glennis pulled me. We were so relieved we got him out. He was covered in toilet sewerage and the smell was so strong, we were all covered in it. All I wanted was to get him home. As we walked through the streets people were crossing over the road to get away from us. We took him home and I explained to his dad that he had thought it was a paddling pool. His dad didn't want to know, he was so angry, and he never thanked us for getting him out. All our parents had to get the tin baths out.

One Saturday we went to the matinee at The Rock. Rita started a fight. I told her to leave it but she couldn't. She arranged to have a fight at the back of St Laurence's Church. I was keeping out of it, when this older lad that I knew from school punched me in my face and ran off. I had two black eyes. I wasn't letting Rita off this time: I punched her in her face and gave her a black eye. I told my dad the truth. On the following Saturday I called for Rita. She thought her mum had gone to work and left her in bed. She was shouting from her bedroom window and asked me to get her something to eat. I went back home to fetch her a dripping sandwich. I put it in a paper bag to take it to her. I told her to open her bedroom window, then I climbed up the drainpipe and squeezed through the small window, giving her the sandwich. Then I heard her mum come back. She shouted up to Rita to get up for her breakfast. Looking at Rita and panicking I said, "What shall I do?" She told me to get back out of the window. I tried to get out but I caught my knickers on the window catch and got stuck. I couldn't reach the drainpipe to climb down. As I was struggling, I slipped. I was hanging by my knickers out of her bedroom window. Some of our neighbours saw me and shouted, "Mary is hanging out of Rita's window, someone get a ladder." It was too late: my knickers gave way and I fell to the pantry roof and, with the shock, I jumped from the pantry roof to the ground. My mum had heard the commotion. I went back home. Mum asked me if I was hurt and I said "no", but I had no knickers - they had ripped and the only part that was left was the elastic round my waist. I didn't get into trouble this time, I got away with it.

That holiday I had learnt to ride the horses: I could rise to the trot and was able to go riding with Jill. I was also speeding around on my roller skates. Dad taught me to weigh a I cwt bag of coal: 1 skip 56 pounds, 2 skips 112 pounds, 112 pounds =1cwt.  He started to teach me how to do his book keeping.  I had done well in Mr Hurtle's class and learnt to do long divisions, short divisions and decimals. The summer holidays were almost over. I was told that I was to be in Mrs Walker's class the next year. She was the strictest teacher in the school. I was hoping to move with my friends into Mrs Heron's class. I suppose it really didn't matter.

I was nine now. Mum said my dad was an alcoholic but the way I saw it Mum and Dad lived in separate rooms: Mum in the kitchen and Dad in the sitting room. Our house had been connected up to the electric and we had light bulbs instead of gas mantles. I was able to see to read as the light bulbs were a lot brighter. I didn't need my torch to read in bed anymore.

Mum bought me a book, "Little Women" by Louisa May Alcott, about four sisters: Meg, Amy, Beth and Jo. I read it over and over again, and many other books such as "Heidi" and "Black Beauty", which made me cry. Mum used to buy us comics every week; I had the "Dandy" and "Beano", Frank had "The Rover" and "Hotspur". We used to swap our comics with our friends. Back in school Mrs Walker was on my case all the time. It was obvious she had heard about my escapades from Mr Jelly; she would bring me out to the front of the whole class and slap my legs with the ruler. If she didn't think I was paying attention she would throw the chalk she was using. To "wake me up" was her excuse. She told me if I didn't show my working out on my maths sheet she was going to mark them wrong. I didn't think I needed to do that as most of the time I could work them out in my head by mental arithmetic. My dad used to teach me his way of doing maths, which was quicker than working it out on paper. What was her problem? Maths was my best subject so I didn't do what she told me to do. She gave me lower grades and put on my school report that I didn't pay attention.

When we were playing out after school one day Rita and Glennis saw a boy we knew hang a cat with my skipping rope and kill it. I was so angry and upset I tied him up with my skipping rope and went over to Dad's garage to get a tow rope. My intention was to frighten him - not to hang him. Rita panicked and ran to fetch his mum. I had tied the tow rope round the old beam that he had used to hang the cat and was making a noose when I heard some screaming and shouting. His mum was running up the yard saying I was going to hang her son. All the neighbours came out and my mum heard the commotion. She came round as well. Brian was untied and his mum took him home. I was in serious trouble; my mum gave me the copper stick and sent me to bed. Brian who had hanged the poor cat got off scot free. I, who only intended to teach him a lesson, got a good hiding. Rita told me she really thought I was going to do it.

Another year was nearly over. I couldn't wait to get out of Mrs Walker's class at the end of term. What a year it had been! After the holidays I would be moving on up into the top class for my final year of the juniors. The six week holidays had come round again. To keep out of trouble I worked with Dad. He gave me part of his garden down the "avenues". I spent hours and days clearing and digging my patch; Dad was amazed how hard I worked. We had "Gerry", an Irish sheepdog that we kept there as a guard dog. I really loved him. We also had "Nigger" - our guard dog at home. Sergeant Wood, the area police officer, gave my dad a summons as we had two dogs but only one licence. One night Sergeant Wood was on his beat, walking towards Dad's coal yard. There was an old horse dray near the fence and there were some broken boards in the fence, leaving a few gaps at the top. I was waiting for Sergeant Wood to come by. I had my catapult and I was good at hitting targets. That night my target was the Sergeant's helmet. I loaded my catapult with a pebble, found the best gap, saw my target and aimed for it. I knocked Sergeant Wood's helmet off. I hid under the horse dray by holding on to the springs. Sergeant Wood came looking for me but didn't catch me. When I saw him go over to our house I went across the school field and climbed back over the wall to our back door. Dad was in the sitting room. I crept through. Dad basically told the Sergeant he'd have to be quick to catch me.

I settled down again; Mum was ill and I had to help more with the housework. I was still helping Dad by weighing up and filling the coal bags in the coal yard for him to take out and deliver. I really believe I should have been born a boy. Working hard had given me strong arm muscles. I honestly didn't know my own strength. I had my own wheelbarrow and could take a bag of coal to an elderly customer that Dad cared about, especially in the winter months.

Going back to school I was happy. I was going into the top class with Mr Dunn - by coincidence my dad delivered his coal. He lived on Windsor Road at the top of Littleworth. In spite of all my distractions I had not done too badly at school. That year I was working towards my 11+ exams, but I was not academically minded. I didn't think I'd pass for grammar school.

I got into trouble on my first day back. Rita was being bullied in the playground. I went to try to stop it. This lad, Roy, kept slapping and kicking Rita. He pulled her on to the ground. I got hold of his clothes and pulled him off Rita; he got up and kicked me. I just got angry and started to fight with him; he was older than me and much bigger but I punched him so hard he reeled over. The poor lad's nose was bleeding. Yes, I won the fight but I wasn't proud of myself. It made me realise fighting back wasn't the answer. When we went back into school my mind was working overtime. Mr Dunn asked me if he could talk to me in confidence. He said, "Mary you can't protect the world, you can't save the world, but you can help to make it a better world." He wasn't just a good teacher, he was right. My last year in the juniors was going too fast. I had taken my 11+ and failed to pass. I chose to go to Ravensdale Secondary School - it was the nearest to home. I was 11 now: I had got to try not to waste the last four years of my education.

# CHAPTER 3

# ON TO SECONDARY SCHOOL

I was very close to my Aunty May, Aunty Nellie and my Uncle Cyril, Dad's sisters and brother. My Aunty May lived on Hope Street, off Bowling Street, just across the road from our home. Aunty Nellie lived on New Market Street. It was called China Town by the locals and very close to the Race Course Park off Eakring Road. Uncle Cyril lived with my dad's mum. He also was a coal merchant and lived across the road from us at 62 Newgate Lane. He and my dad used to share the family coal yard and garages. My grandad Crowder died when I was six; I remember standing on the front of my grandma's house watching the funeral. The hearse was drawn by six black horses, the undertakers sat up high and the driver was wearing a large black top hat and a black suit with tails. He held a long black horse whip in his hand and there were three horse-drawn carriages following. My grandad was the last of our family to have a horse-driven funeral. My grandma was very strict. She was a big woman who worked hard in the coal yard and was very strong. I must admit I was frightened of her. I made sure I never got on the wrong side of her. She would have had "my guts for garters" - an expression she used.

I was now 11 in the summer holidays, 1950. My little sister, Jacqueline, was four years old. I loved her to bits, she was so pretty. I took her with me at every chance I had. My friends didn't mind me taking her along. We used to go down the avenues with jars to catch grasshoppers. I think they are also called crickets, little green insects that jump through the air. We didn't hurt them; we used to see who caught the most then let them go again.

We would also watch the trains pass by; the train drivers would wave to us. We decided we would go to Carr Bank Park to play on the swings, slide and see-saws. Our mums would pack us up a picnic sometimes and we would play out all day. I was also going to riding lessons - I loved riding. I made a new friend, Nita. She had lots of experience as she had been riding since she was four. Nita was the same age as me. The horses I was allowed to ride were Pippin, a little black pony, Lady, a little bay, and Fiona who was 14 hands high. Nita's horse, Tosco, was 16 hands. We used to go riding through Woodhouse and take the back lanes up to Garibaldi near Forest Town to give the horses a good exercise. Nita told me she was going to Ravensdale School. She lived on Newgate Lane next to King Street, close to St Laurence's Church. That meant we could walk to school together. I went swimming and made another new friend at the baths, Sylvia. We used to race against each other. She was older than me and a very strong swimmer. She lived on Newton Street. She attended the Queen Elizabeth Grammar School. Mum decided to let Jacqueline go to the baths with us provided I always made sure she was safe. I had shortened my sister's name to Jacky, which Mum didn't like. Most of my friends called her Jacky, anyway. One day at the baths a boy pushed Jacky in the pool before I had time to put on her safety ring. I had to jump in and get her out. She was winded when he pushed her in and it frightened her; she wouldn't go again for a long time.

Dad often took us to Mr and Mrs Halifax's farm at Hockerton, near Southwell. Dad used to trade them coal in exchange for farm butter, cheese, eggs, rabbits, etc. We would also help on the farm with sugar beeting, hoeing and milking and Dad would call at the Spread Eagle pub on our way home. I would get crisps and pop. Tom, their son, let me drive the tractor sometimes; the seat was metal and uncomfortable. Dad also arranged some music lessons for me with Mrs Humphrey on Carisbrooke Avenue near Crown Farm. I used to go for one hour every week. I did learn to play the piano just enough for my own amusement.

I didn't go to work with my dad much that summer and spent some time with my mum. She took us on the train to Mablethorpe. We went from the railway station on Central Road - the LNER. The other railway in Mansfield was the Midland. On the journey back from Mablethorpe it was dark. There were lights on the train but they were very dim. The adults started talking about ghosts - I suppose it was the atmosphere on the train. I felt a bit scared and was pleased to get home.

The last week of the holidays I had managed to keep out of trouble, apart from when we went scrumping up on Eakring Road. There were a lot of big houses with orchards close to the main road. Frank was with us; he pushed me off the wall and I fell into the garden. Frank had got me into trouble again but Dad sorted it out.

Starting at Ravensdale School I was put into Miss Feery's class, with pupils who had come from Forest Town. She gave us a maths test and I got all mine right. "Where is your working out?" she asked. I tried to explain that I did it in my head but she was really angry with me. She accused me of copying. I ran out of the class really upset and bumped into another teacher, Miss Rice, who took me into an empty classroom to talk to me. She put me some sums on the board. They were harder sums than my year, but I did them. She said she would sort it out. I didn't want to go back into my class and Miss Rice arranged for me to sit in her class for maths until things could be sorted. I was transferred to Mrs Packer's class. She was a PE teacher and I excelled in PE and games. Mr Davis took us for art, Mr Daniels for science and Mrs Robinson for cookery. After a bad start I settled down with Mrs Packer. At playtimes and lunch I met up with my friends from Newgate Lane. I stayed for school dinners. They were good meals and good puddings; there were always seconds if we wanted them. Mrs Buttery was the dinner lady, she knew my mum and dad and she was always nice - she always had a kind word for everybody.

It was coming up to Christmas. Dad had started drinking again and he and Mum were arguing. I walked in from school when Mum was shouting at Dad, telling him the son he was paying maintenance for could not come to our house. She didn't want us to know we had another brother. Dad said if it had not been for his mum interfering he would have married the girl he was engaged to. They weren't aware that I had overheard their conversation. Mum packed her case and again went to stay with Grandma, taking Jacky and Frank with her, leaving me at home with Dad knowing I would keep the house clean. I really felt sorry for them both; I wasn't old enough to do anything.

I begged Dad to give up drinking. I cried and told him I didn't want him to kill himself with the drink. Dad worked hard: he always got up for work even if he had been drunk the night before. When he came home from work he would send me to fetch his beer from the off licence on Ratcliffe Gate next to Mr and Mrs West's fish and chip shop. The off licence was not allowed to let me bring out beer unless it had a label over the top of the bottle to protect licensing laws. I fetched Dad's beer most nights. I was going to school, cleaning the house, cooking meals for me and Dad and I was still only eleven. My school life was being affected by my home life. I am so pleased that Jacky wasn't old enough for it to affect her. I did think that if things didn't change, then Jacky would be affected. That Christmas was one of the worst I can remember, we were a family split up. Dad tried to get Mum back - he begged her to come home. Mum just couldn't trust him, his promises were like pie crusts - he always broke them. I sometimes wonder how I kept going. Dad did buy me a new bike for Christmas and I know he sent the money to Mum to buy Frank and Jacky's presents. He also gave my mum money for herself. It was February before Mum came back home; Dad had tried giving up the drink so that she would return. Things went back to normal again. However, Frank was back with his lies and cheating and causing trouble between me and Mum.

The year seemed to be dragging, thank God I had Jacky. I just wanted to protect her while I could. Moving on to my next year I was now 12. Mr Davis was my teacher. It was a better year for me at school. In domestic science we were being taught how to clean and scrub everything as we used it. It was mainly about health and hygiene. We were then taught to bake, cook and make pastry. I got good marks and that encouraged me to follow my recipe to the book. My first cakes were fairy cakes - not good. I used the wrong flour and the cakes went flat. At the weekend I took Jacky to the Rock Cinema with me. I spent the last of my pocket money on ice cream at Lee's shop on Skerry Hill. On passing a grocery shop further down Jacky wanted an apple. I told her no, I had no money left. I was walking just in front. When we got round the corner at the bottom of King Street, I could hear a crunching sound. I looked behind me and Jacky was crunching on a giant carrot; she had picked it up off the box at the front of the grocery shop where the fruit and veg were on display. My friends thought it was funny. I couldn't go back and pay for it and I didn't dare take it back. I told Jacky that she must never do that again. At least she enjoyed the carrot!

When I went to school on my bike I used to give Rita a "backy" on the saddle. We were coming down Pecks Hill one night after school when I realised my brakes were faulty; I had to stop the bike with my shoes. Imagine my shock when the toe caps were hanging off and badly scuffed; I knew I would be in trouble. I must admit it taught me a lesson not to give "backies" coming down the hill again.

I managed to do well at school and was given a place to go to a boarding school for a month. Dad paid for me to go and Nita also got a place. We went to Amber Valley boarding school in Derbyshire. It was absolutely great. We all slept in a wooden dormitory - there were separate toilets, showers, wash basins, a medical centre and classrooms. We did a lot of nature studies and looked after animals, as well as normal lessons. There was a large cookhouse and dining room. We sat singing round the camp fires. We absolutely had a great time - Amber Valley, what happy memories!

That year went far too fast. I was 13 and all through the summer holiday I worked with Dad. I could now use my shovel to load the lorry, help Dad with furniture removals, lift plaster boards, carry bags of plaster and cement, and my hands were as rough as sandpaper from loading bricks onto the lorry. I was just like a lad and dressed like a lad, with a leather helmet to protect my hair. At the pit, loading the lorry, we had to share the coal truck with other coal merchants. One of Orchard's drivers pulled up by the side of us. I noticed that the lad with him was the lad that had blacked my eyes a few years before. When he got on to the platform of the truck I picked up my shovel and I was going to hit him with it. My dad managed to grab the shovel and stop me from hitting him. My dad had already caught on and seemed to know. The driver moved off to share another truck, he obviously didn't trust me with the shovel. Some of the other drivers thought it was funny. The lad was frightened. I didn't think he'd pick on anyone again.

Dad brought me a Singer treadle sewing machine. I wanted to learn to make dresses and help Mum to make some new curtains. I very quickly learnt how to load the shuttle and change the cotton and needles. Mum used it as well. Jacky was going to tap dancing lessons at the Gabriel Osborne School of Dancing. Dad had bought her a pogo stick; she was a natural at her dancing and a wizard on the pogo stick. I don't know how she kept her balance, she was so good. One of her friends, David, was also good; they went up and down the street, effortlessly. I stuck to my roller skates. Hula hoops were also all the rage, but not my thing. My friends on Haywood Street had an old penny farthing bike that had been in their family for many years, handed down. How they could ride it was a mystery to me.

I made a go-cart out of wood: I put in a seat, two pushchair wheels at the front and two pram wheels at the back and I bolted on a steering bar for my feet. I put the poker into the fire till it was red hot, then burnt two holes, one each side of the steering bar, to tie a pull rope so I could control the go-cart with my hands and feet.

Dad helped me to put a brake on it in case it went too fast. All my pals wanted a go. Most of our school life was making our own fun. I also made a sledge for the snow. Dad put some metal runners on it to make it go faster. One boy got killed while sledging on Rayner's - he had the kind of sledge where you stood on the back. The sledge hit some metal railings and he was thrown up on to the spikes.

It was an eventful year. We had a good Mischievous Night - we tied the door knobs together of neighbours on Bowling Street, Arthur Street and Frederick Street, all in the one night. Our friends all joined in. We got chased, shouted at and told off; it was all in fun. The next night was Bonfire Night; we had made our own Guy Fawkes and made lamps out of turnips. My aunty Nellie made toffee apples, roast potatoes and roast chestnuts. There were fireworks - Catherine wheels, jumping Jacks, bangers, rockets, volcanoes and many more. These events happened every year throughout my life. I was coming up to 14, my last year at school. I was planning on joining my dad and working in the business when I left school but Mum had other ideas.

I moved up into Mr Daniels' class. Our classroom was the science lab. We were taught to blow glass by heating up the glass on Bunsen burners, then blowing it into shapes and letting it cool down once we had moulded it. I was in the hockey team that year. We were practising on Sherwood Hall Road field. I was playing centre forward. I was so eager to score a goal I brought my stick up too high and knocked out one of my classmates. The teacher called sticks but it was too late. Marlene was laid out on the field with a lump on her forehead, just like the lump on my brother's head the time I hit him with the poker. I felt so bad although this was an accident. I can't imagine how her parents felt.

That year was the year when I was going to have to grow up and take some responsibility. Frank had left school and he didn't want to go to work. He went on to the milk rounds with Maw's Dairy on Southwell Road but that didn't last long. He took other jobs but he just couldn't cope, so Mum and Dad were having to support him. Jacky was seven and moving up to the Juniors at Newgate Lane. It was the year of the Queen's coronation, 1953. We didn't have television. I used to babysit for two neighbours, Barbara and Denis, who owned the home bakery and shop on Newgate Lane. Terry and Mary had a fruit and veg shop at the bottom of Bowling Street, across the road from our house. They both had 12 inch black and white televisions. I watched the coronation with Terry and Mary. The neighbours all joined together to put on a big party, including a fancy dress competition. I was a gypsy with long plaits that Mum made out of wool. Jacky was a fairy with the wings attached to her dress; Mum made her a silver wand. Every child was given a coronation crown. There were celebrations but nothing compared to my Victory Day memories.

I didn't get out with my friends much during that summer holiday. I was either cleaning for Mum, working for Dad or babysitting. The money earned I put aside for my riding lessons. Mum started taking Jacky for ice skating lessons at the Nottingham Ice Stadium. I only managed to go the once with Mum and Jacky.

Then I was fifteen, in my last week of my school life. I had already had to get a job - starting at Forster, Clay and Ward's on the Monday after the Friday I left school.

**Me and my sister, Jackie, in 1952**

# CHAPTER 4

# FAMILY TRAGEDY

I went to bed and cried. My heart was broken. My mum was going to leave my dad if he took me on working for him. She told him I had been a lad too long and that she wanted me in dresses; she told Dad to let me grow up to be more feminine. It was time for him to let me go and live a normal girl's life.

I hated the factory. I worked hard and I tipped up my wages to my mum and believe me, I couldn't tell anyone how I felt. I don't know how Dad felt. He never showed his feelings. When I wasn't at work, and Mum was out, I would help Dad with his book keeping. I felt for my dad, I could see how depressed he was. Drinking was the only thing holding him together. Mum was suffering every time she came in, Dad was angry, aggressive and abusive. Frank had gone into the army. Jacky and I were both victims of a broken marriage. My mum would go out to the Carpenter's Arms where she made friends with the landlady, Fran. Mum sang and played the piano most weekends and she was also baking cakes for the customers. When she wasn't there she was at my grandma's with the family. My aunty Gladys asked my mum to let me go with her and my cousins for a week's holiday in Blackpool to give me a break. Aunty Gladys knew my situation and really felt for me. Mum was being led by her brother, Uncle Bill, and his wife, Aunty Helen. She was a very kind, caring lady. I liked her; she was good to my mum.

On the holiday I met Aunty Dorothy and Uncle Clarry. They owned the Marina Hotel on St Chads Road in Blackpool. Aunty Gladys must have told them about my life. After a lovely week's holiday, when we were leaving to come home, Aunty Dorothy put her arms round me and gave me a big hug. I had never, ever had a hug in my whole life. I must have gone bright red with the embarrassment. I didn't know how to deal with it. Aunty Dorothy told me to come back and visit, and I could also bring a friend with me. She told me to ring her if I ever needed to talk.

When I got home I was afraid to discuss my feelings with anyone. Uncle Bill and Aunty Helen left Mansfield, taking Grandma with them. They got the Masons Arms pub in Old Basford, near Nottingham. At the weekends they asked me and my cousins, Judy and Vera, to help them out. We used to go when we could: collecting the glasses, cleaning out ashtrays, sweeping and mopping floors.

Aunty Helen looked after us well but I couldn't go every weekend.

Mum and Dad were growing further and further apart. I had to go down the garden to weigh up the bags of coal for Dad to deliver. He needed me and I felt I couldn't let him down. He carried on working and earning the best he could. There was no way he could turn his life round. He was an alcoholic. Nothing I or anyone else could do would change things. Grandma and Uncle Cyril tried to help him, but Dad just wouldn't listen - he was killing himself. Mum was out with her friends or going over to Basford to be with my grandma. I was feeling more and more isolated and felt I was losing my sister. Both of us were torn. Jacky had witnessed my dad kicking my mum under the table. Frank came home; he had gone AWOL from the army. Mum took him in. He was hiding in the bedroom when the military police surrounded our house. My brother tried to escape through the bedroom window; he got arrested and taken back to the army. That caused so much trouble for Mum. Dad said Mum must never let Frank back into the house under any circumstances.

At work, Mr Lyman who did the book keeping in the mending room was having a problem with the books. I sorted out the problem for him. He gave me another job working with him alongside the women in the mending room. I loved listening to their stories and hearing them singing some of the old songs that were around before I was born. They got short of staff in the knitting room and I was transferred to train on the machine sewing buttons on cardigans. I was on my own time and earning good wages when some of the girls started messing around. The end result of their messing around was that I lost my temper and punched the ring leader. I got the sack. I had been there over a year and I was 16 now.

Mum was angry with me but Dad told me not to worry: "While ever you've got a pair of hands and are willing to work, you'll get a job." I got one straight away. I went to work for the Co-op Dairy delivering milk on the milk rounds. I was up early in the mornings and by lunchtime we'd finished for the day. My cousin, Lilian, told me there was a vacancy at the ABC Cinema for an usherette. I decided to go for it and got the job. The hours were from 1pm to 10pm: that suited me. I was doing two jobs and bringing home two wages and still tipping up to my mum. She used to give me ten shillings a week back in pocket money. I didn't need much with working all hours. I got promoted at the cinema to Head Sales Girl. I was put in charge over the usherettes and could call on them to help me during the intervals. The manageress, Miss Wragg, became my friend. She used make sure we both had the same day off so that I could help her to move house. She lived on Nottingham Road with her mum.

When her mum passed away she moved to Sherburn Avenue off Bath Lane. When she was away relieving at other cinemas in Nottingham or Chesterfield she would leave me the key to look after her house. She was good to me. Mr Dunn, the door man, and his wife, Margery, used to invite me to their home on Carisbrooke Avenue for dinner or tea. Mr Dunn saved me the posters from Tommy Steele films - he was my favourite teenage crush. I used to stick Tommy's posters all over my bedroom wall. Miss Wragg invited me to the Metropol Cinema in Sherwood, Nottingham, to see the film "The Story of Esther Costello", a young girl who found an unexploded bomb in a derelict building after the war. It went off and killed her friends; she was left deaf, dumb and blind. Miss Wragg came to find me in the interval and brought me a box of paper handkerchiefs. I was sobbing my heart out, emotional over the film!

At the age of 17 I left the dairy and the cinema to become a conductress on the Mansfield traction buses. The wages were good and I soon picked up the fares, stages, routes and destinations. Kath trained me and we became good friends. I made many friends and not only at the depot. Working with the people and public was my dream job. I saved up and bought myself a little 50cc BSA Bantam motorbike from Henstock's on Chesterfield Road near Bull Farm, to get me to and from work. I worked many double shifts, there was always loads of overtime if you wanted it. I was on the pit runs, service runs and long distance runs. If I was on a split shift I would go to the canteen for a meal, or join in with a game of cards or snooker with the other duckies. Dad would shout me up to make sure I didn't miss my shift, and wait up for me if I was on lates. When I was on the Crown Farm or Forest Town Run on a Sunday shift, Dad would wait on our doorstep with a jug of tea for me and the driver. We would pick Dad up outside our front door on our way up and drop him back off on our return journey. I was still helping Miss Wragg out at the cinema when the operatics were staging their musicals and needed extra staff. I would help Aunty Helen and Uncle Bill out if I got a weekend off. I could work the beer pumps, serve drinks and change the barrels now. I had a very busy life. My friends from the buses would take me for a night out in Nottingham, dancing at the Palace or for a pub crawl. I had met a boy named Barry who wanted to take me out. I was his friend and that is how it stayed; I didn't want a relationship. My dad was strict: he wouldn't let me take a boy home.

I still did my share of the housework and still helped Dad when I could. One day Dad came home, falling over everywhere, shouting and swearing. Mum was going to Grandma's with Jacky and I decided to go with Mum, hoping Dad would go to bed and sleep it off. We had got as far as the railway station on Central Road when we heard someone shouting us back. It was Emma, our window cleaner. She said my dad was hurt. I ran home as fast as I could. I went through the door: my dad was sat at the table with his hand over his face with blood pouring through his fingers. I felt sick and thought I was going to pass out. Mum and Jacky weren't far behind me. Frank, who we hadn't seen since his arrest by the MPs, had called to try to get into the house for some money. He had forced the door, knocking Dad over. He had kicked Dad in the face, then ran off. We thought Dad had lost his eye. I sat in the chair, crying. I wished I'd stayed at home. Dad told me not to cry, he would be alright. That didn't make me feel any better.

A few nights later I came home off late shift and went to bed. I wasn't asleep. I had put the light out when I heard the doorknob of my bedroom door turning. The door didn't open but I saw the figure of a lady float past me. She then floated to the side of my bed, looked down at me and smiled. I pinched myself to see if I was dreaming: I wasn't. I just screamed out, "There's a ghost in my room." Mum didn't believe me but, as God is my judge, I know what I saw.

I had been on the buses for over two years now: I was 19. I used to go out with my friend, Ray. Her dad was a coal merchant on the corner of Broxtowe Drive and Prospect Street. She had a little MG car. We had been up to Crown

Pit and one of the deputies, Bill, took us down the pit to show us what it was like for the miners. We went on the coal face training section; we saw the trepanning machine that cut the coal and the sandbags and props. We crawled on our hands and knees; we had a safety helmet with a lamp on the front. While we were down the pit I had a weird sensation: I felt a fear I couldn't understand. I didn't tell anyone.

It was dark when Ray dropped me off back at home. After Ray drove off I saw Mum on the front with Jacky and Nelly from next door. Mum was frightened; she was afraid to go in the house. She told me she had heard Dad shouting and swearing at someone. I looked through the letterbox. I couldn't hear anything and I couldn't see Dad sat at the table where he usually sat if he was up. I asked Mum to unlock the door to let me in. Everything was quiet and Dad had gone to bed. I told Mum, "Dad won't hurt you, let's go to bed." The next morning I remember Dad calling me up for work. I was on a split shift that day. I was going to go to the canteen for my break and I felt something was wrong. I could feel a tight pulling on my heart that I had only felt once in my life before, and that was when Dad got hurt. I knew I had to go home. When I arrived home there were two cars outside our house. I went through the door and saw our doctor, another man and Mum in the living room standing near the table. I knew something was terribly wrong. I saw the door to the cellar was open. I ran to the cellar. Uncle Cyril was coming up the cellar steps. I ran down the cellar pushing past Uncle Cyril. He tried to hold me back. I saw my dad laid on the floor on a sack. Dad wasn't moving, his face looked like stone. I got down on to the floor and took hold of his hand: it was cold. I tried rubbing his hands to make them warm. The doctor had come down the cellar and he tried to console me. My dad was dead; he had committed suicide by hanging himself.

He had paid for a holiday for me only the week before. Miss Wragg had booked this holiday for us on an overland tour of Austria. I could not talk to my mum. I had to stay at home to sort out the business, audit the books and collect in money owed to Dad from contracts. Mum had never dealt with any of this. Uncle Cyril sold off Dad's lorries and he gave the money to Mum. Now Dad had gone I had taken on the responsibility of being the bread winner. Dad had been putting away money for me in war bonds - savings I couldn't cash in until I reach the age of 21. Aunty Dorothy heard about Dad; she asked me to go over to Blackpool and told me I could take a friend. I took Glennis with me for a week. It was only a month after losing Dad. Aunty Dorothy and Uncle Clarry took us to shows and dancing at the Tower Ballroom. Uncle Clarry took us to a football match between Blackpool and Everton. They gave us both hugs as we were leaving. Aunty Dorothy told me they loved me and that they would always be there for me if I ever needed them. Two weeks after that I went to Austria with Miss Wragg. It was the first time I had been on a plane. We visited Luxemburg, France, Oberammagau, Austria and the Tyrol. It was a wonderful holiday.

I couldn't get over Dad's death, it wasn't Mum's fault. I decided I wanted to go into the army - I wanted to run away. Mum didn't want me to go. I went to Nottingham to the Army Careers office. I took the tests for maths, arithmetic and English: I passed the tests with 84%. The officer told me that, once I was posted after the medical, I should consider taking advantage of the army's further education. I passed my medical with no problems. I was taken to a room where there was a picture of the Queen on the wall. I had to swear an oath, while saluting, to serve my Queen and country. Two weeks later I got notification that I was to report to the army training camp at Guildford in Surrey on the 26th December, 1959. In with the notification was a one way travel warrant from Mansfield to Guildford. That meant my last day at home would be Christmas Day. My mum was upset. So that she wouldn't struggle financially I signed my War Savings Certificates over to her. I agreed that most of my army pay could be paid to her, so that she could draw it from the Post Office. I just couldn't leave my mum and Jacky to struggle. All my friends from the bus depot threw a party for me in Nottingham. They got me a record - Tommy Bruce, singing "Ain't Misbehavin". After three years as a bus conductress, at the age of 20, I was on my way to a new life in the army.

# CHAPTER 5

# MY ARMY LIFE

My mum and Jacky were still in bed when I left home early on Boxing Day morning. In a way it saved me having to say my goodbyes. I went to Nottingham on the bus, on to the station to catch the train to London, and then changed again to take a bus to Guildford. On arriving at Guildford there were two army corporals waiting with some other new recruits, with an army bus ready to take us to the training camp.

On arrival it was all go - we were registered and put into three groups. I was put into B platoon. We were taken to our accommodation, a wooden dormitory with a separate ablution block for 18 of us who would be doing our training together for the next five weeks. We were introduced to our training officers, Corporal Scott and Corporal Degarry-Martin. Then we went to the stores to be issued with all our kit: one khaki battle dress uniform with two khaki shirts, a tie, one pair of brown leather shoes, two pairs of tan stockings, one green beret, one bottle- green No. 1 dress uniform, with two white shirts, one green tie, two pairs of black stockings, one pair of black shoes, one green peaked hat, and a green shoulder bag. On the top of all this we got a full PE kit and a khaki greatcoat, bath towels and bedding. I kept thinking, "How much more!"

From day one it was all action: cleaning, bulling up our shoes till they looked like glass, physical training in the gym, drill - learning to march with the whole platoon - and getting up before dawn if we wanted breakfast. The army food was good - I used to eat like a horse. Believe me, I was healthy and fit. To top it all we were put in competition with the other platoons. Corporal Scott intended us to win the cups for the best at PE and drill. One day while we were out on drill practising marching on the spot, she called me to stand with her to watch the platoon. She halted them and said, "Watch me." She marched on the spot, bringing her knees up very high as an example. Then she yelled at the platoon, "Can you see my drawers?"

The platoon answered, "No, corporal."

She replied, looking at me, "No, we can't see yours, so lift up them knees," then sent me back to my place in the platoon. I really did respect her.

Just before the drill contest I was called out again by Corporal Scott to watch the platoon marching. She then asked me what I thought. I said, "Good." She looked at me with a frown. She told me I needed glasses, and then said, "I think they look like marching penguins." I knew she was doing this to make the platoon work harder. It worked. Our platoon won both cups and the "best platoon of the intake".

Then came the passing out ceremony. Our training was over and we were given our postings. I was being sent to Northern Ireland to join the Royal Signals regiment. My mum didn't make it to the passing out parade. I had been going to church on Sundays. The Padre had asked me to forgive God for the way my father had died and to retake my confirmation before leaving Guildford. I was confirmed and blessed by the Bishop of London in my No.1 dress uniform. I didn't get home on leave after my training: my posting was to be immediate. My address would be Thiepval Barracks, Lisbon, County Antrim, near Belfast. The army had sorted out my train tickets to Heysham and my ferry to Belfast. The boat I crossed on was named the "Duke of Argyle". The army had also booked me a berth. I met another girl who had joined the army; she was in the Alexander Nursing Corps. The sea was rough and the boat was rocking everywhere. The other young girl was so sick I gave her my berth so she could lie down. Up on deck I met two soldiers; they were from Ireland and were coming home on leave. One of the soldiers, Neil, asked me for my name and my army postal address so he could write to me.

I arrived in Belfast early in the morning. When I got off the boat an army officer was waiting to take me to the barracks. She took me to my block, showed me my bed and left. It was a Saturday morning and everything was quiet. The girls I was with were asleep; they had been on nights manning the phones. I went to have a look round and met a soldier from the Royal Engineers. He told me his name was Eric and he was a cook in the kitchens. He showed me round the camp and took me to the NAAFI. He told me he was a sergeant as he was not in uniform. He said most of the camp only worked Monday to Friday with every weekend off - that was why everybody was having a sleep-in. I thanked him and went back to my block. A girl came to talk to me, she was still in her pyjamas. She told me she was the camp's nurse in the Alexandra Nursing Corps. Her name was Doreen, her rank a corporal. She got dressed and took me up to the sergeants' mess. I had my uniform on and questioned if I was allowed in the sergeants' mess. She told me it was no problem as long as we were friends. Another girl came in, she was in uniform, I could see she was also a corporal. Her name was Gwen; she was a Welsh girl in the Royal Signals like me. We soon became friends.

I asked Doreen if there was a firing range on the camp; she told me that she would take me up on Sunday after I had settled in. Doreen took me to the firing range as she promised. I was lying on the floor on my stomach, firing at the target, when a lady with a boxer dog spoke to me. She said to watch I didn't get a kick from the gun, if I hadn't used a gun before. She wound my score board to look at, smiled and said, "Not bad, carry on."

I said to Doreen, "You went quiet, who is she?"

Doreen said, "You will find out tomorrow, that's Captain Bray."

The next day I was taken to Captain Bray's office; she made me welcome then sent me to see Sergeant Major Campbell as I would be working with him in the stores. I decided that with the weekends free I would take advantage of the army education. The teachers were so laid back and helpful. I put in to take higher grades in maths, English and map reading. I had made another new friend, she was my sergeant major. I used to perm her hair with home perms like Twink. She trained me to take drill in camp on the large square where parades were held. Captain Bray got me some babysitting jobs with families that lived in army accommodation houses to earn me extra money; she knew my wages were going to help my mum. She also used me and my friends to help out with the waiting in the officers' mess on big occasions, sometimes passing me and my friends a drink now and again.

On Friday nights on our block it was active. The men's quarters were above ours and the men would send their shirts down to us on coat hangers tied to a rope for us to iron. We would send our shoes back up to them to bull and polish for us. It was all good fun. Sergeant Major Campbell used to ask me to go to Eric in the cook house for milk if we ran out, and he sent Eric a Stay Bright badge in return. With the babysitting I was looking after twins for the sergeant and his wife with no problems. Captain Bray told me she had another job for me to do. It was for the Commanding Secretary of the camp. He lived in Belfast and had five young boys. He used to pick me up after work on Friday. I would babysit Friday and Saturday nights and they used to take me out with them and the children on Sundays. I had my own bedroom when I stayed. I was allowed to do my washing and ironing and to help myself if I wanted anything to eat. I didn't abuse their trust, they were good to me and paid me well. I was also allowed to go back to work with him on Monday mornings, excused from morning dress parade.

I had been in the army a year before I got a leave home. I had saved most of my babysitting money. I couldn't wait to see Jacky. I got presents for her: a new watch and some Irish chocolate. Jacky had written and asked me if I could get home in time to meet her outside her school in my uniform. Jacky was at High Oakham School. I didn't let her down; I went to meet her in my No.1 dress uniform - she was so proud of me! I enjoyed my leave. Aunty Dorothy and Uncle Clarry managed to get down from

Blackpool to see me. Mum was proud of me too, I know she was. I gave her some extra money from what I had saved to help her out.

When it was time for me to return to camp I was looking forward to being back with my mates. When I got back to camp I found out that I had passed all my further education and my map reading exams. The teacher wanted me to go up another level. I said I would think about it. I could do almost every job in the camp and would help out where I was needed. I had even been working in the telephone exchange for Gwen, putting through calls. Doreen, Gwen and I were soulmates: nothing was ever going to split us up. One day we were off work and going up to the sergeants' mess. We were walking along the corridor on the block, the three of us arm in arm, kicking up our legs and singing the song, "Sisters". We had been told we must always walk orderly through the corridors. Suddenly, round the corner walked our sergeant major. She just looked at us and said, "Carry on girls, it's nice to see you are happy."

Captain Bray sent for me; she had a new working uniform for me to try on - it was replacing the old Battle Dress uniform. It was a smart working uniform similar to the Women's Air Force uniform, only green. It was size 12 and fitted me perfectly. Captain Bray told me there was an exhibition in Belfast and we were taking part. There was going to be a big parade through Belfast. I was to be in the march, then change out of the old uniform and into the new one to stand on show at the exhibition, where I was to encourage young girls to join up. I loved all the pomp and ceremony of the march through Belfast with the big bands playing. I was on a stand with the Grenadier Guards. I wanted a photo taken wearing one of their busbies. A guardsman told me that if I was brave enough to go on the parachute jump I could try on his busby. I did the parachute jump but when I got back to the stand he'd gone.

Back in camp we were told we had a big admin parade coming up. I had to help Staff Sergeant Major Campbell get all the stores ready. We were told we had a pre-admin parade at 14.00 hours on the Wednesday. I forgot all about it until Captain Bray came into the stores. I was painting the shelves and she asked me why I'd missed the pre-admin parade. I looked at my watch and said, "It's not 4 o'clock yet ma'am." She picked up a paint brush and helped me to finish the painting, then told me to put the kettle on for a cup of tea. As we were drinking our tea she told me to rethink army time. The penny suddenly dropped: 14.00 hours was 2 o'clock!

The admin parade went well and we were chosen as the best camp. Major Waller gave us a day off for all our hard work. I wanted to go into Belfast to do some shopping for toiletries. I was outside the guard house when Captain Bray pulled up in her car. "Where are you going?" she asked. I told her I was going into Belfast and she told me to jump into her car. She was going to Belfast and might as well give me a lift. I collected the stores' champ vehicle at the depot to collect some bedding for Staff Sergeant Major. On my way to the stores I saw one of the army heavy trucks on the square. The lads started to mess about; they caught my back wheel and tipped me over. All I could do was wrap my legs round the steering column. The champ went over and over. When it stopped I crawled out. Captain Bray was looking very concerned but the champ wasn't too damaged and I had been lucky. I was told to get back into the vehicle. I couldn't. Captain Bray told me I would never drive again unless I got straight back in. She was right, I had to lose the fear of rolling over.

A few weeks later I received a letter from my mum. Inside it was a letter from her doctor telling me my mum was very ill with terminal cancer and I should seriously consider a compassionate discharge as she needed me back at home. I needed someone to talk to. I went to my sergeant major who told me that I should talk to Captain Bray. I gave her the doctor's letter from my mum. She asked how old my sister was, I said, "14 in July." Captain Bray said she felt that I should get a compassionate discharge. My friend Doreen had gone home on leave but

Gwen was upset for me. I was given leave to go home. When I arrived home I had to see Major Vallance. He owned the printing company on Burns Street in Mansfield. He understood how I felt. He put my compassionate discharge straight through.

I had been in the army one year and seven months. I had to go back over to Ireland to hand all my kit in and say goodbye to my friends. The sergeant major had been like a mother to me, and Captain Bray - what can I say? One of the best friends I ever had. When I was leaving the camp and saying my goodbyes, the sergeant major was crying. I cried, too, on the journey home. The army kept me on their payroll until November 1961, 4 months later.

**A photo of me when I was in the WRAC**

# CHAPTER 6

# MY MUM'S BATTLE WITH CANCER

My mum was very poorly, she was suffering a lot of pain. I had got four months' pay from the army back holiday pay that I had not taken, and from credits that I had accumulated. ("Credits" were money that the army put in for us to help to replace worn out or damaged uniforms. I hadn't had to replace anything; I looked after my kit so my credits had mounted up.) I didn't have to look for work right away. I had been back home for three weeks when Mum went to the hospital for a check up on how far the cancer had spread. It was bad news and Mum was going to have to have an operation. I decided to go back on the buses to earn some extra money, to make sure Mum could get the things she needed to go into hospital. Aunty Helen was helping us with Mum and bringing her some home-made soups and fresh fruit, although Mum wasn't eating a lot and she was losing weight. I noticed my mum's lips were blue and her skin was yellow. Mum was very worried about the operation but the doctors had said it was necessary. Aunty Helen took Jacky home with her when Mum went into the hospital. Mum told me I was to give Aunty Helen my wages and Aunty Helen would pay the bills and do the shopping. I didn't argue, although I knew I was quite capable of running the house. I stayed at home and went to work.

Mum's operation was a colostomy, so she had to have a bag on her side. I went to visit her with Aunty Helen after the operation. Mum had all these tubes and pipes attached to her. I could smell the anaesthetic when I stood near her bed. I had a funny ringing in my ears and I felt dizzy. The next I remember I was sat in a chair and being given some smelling salts by a nurse: I had passed out! Aunty Helen said she wouldn't bring me again if I was going to pass out. Mum was in hospital a long time. When she came home she had to go to Nottingham City Hospital for radiotherapy, but nothing worked. The doctors did not tell my mum how ill she was and I didn't tell Jacky.

It was around now that Barry, the boy I met before going into the army, started to call for me, wanting me to go out with him. I came home from work one day and he was sat with my mum. He had been keeping her company and making her drinks. This went on for a while. One night after work he asked me to marry him. I had never thought of getting married. Mum said to me, "Why don't you marry Barry? I don't think I've got long and I'd like to see you married before I go; it would make me happy to know you've got someone." I wasn't ready to get settled down, I hadn't thought of any future. Mum was getting frailer and I could see her skin turning yellow; I was frightened for her. I agreed to marry Barry to give her something to live for.

We set the date for my 23rd birthday: March 29th, 1962. Aunty Dorothy and Uncle Clarry came down from Blackpool. We had the Drill Hall on Bath Street for our reception. Jacky was one of my bridesmaids, along with one of Barry's cousins. When the photographs were taken, Mum was so weak that Aunty Helen and Aunty Gladys had to hold her up. Aunty Helen, Aunty Dorothy and Uncle Clarry did all the food and waiting on. It was a lovely wedding. Mum paid for the reception and I paid for all the dresses, flowers and rings. Barry's family was struggling but his dad paid for the church and cars. I liked Barry's dad, he was a hard worker and a pay clerk at Welbeck Colliery. His mum was too soft with Barry and covered up for him - I learnt that almost immediately.

We stayed with Mum. Out of the blue, my brother, Frank, turned up on our doorstep with his wife, Barbara. She was expecting a baby. They had a flat in Woodhouse. As ill as Mum was she took to Barbara, and Jacky and I got on well with her too. She had a little girl and they named her Susan. When I came home from work one day my mum was upset. Barbara's mum was there as well and she was crying. She had gone to visit Barbara, who had come home from the hospital with the baby. Frank had locked her in the flat and burnt all her clothes and wouldn't open the door. I borrowed some clothes for Barbara, went down to their flat and knocked on the door. I could hear Barbara crying. I shouted to Frank, "You had better open this door or I promise you I will kick it down." With that Frank opened the door. Barbara was stood in there with just a coat wrapped round her. I passed her the clothes and told her to get dressed - I was taking her home with me. She got dressed and I told Barbara to get the baby. Frank looked at me and said, "She's going nowhere." I told him I was taking Barbara and the baby with me and not to try to stop us leaving. We got to the bus stop and Frank came running behind us. We got on the bus and Frank tried to jump on the platform. I brought my foot up and kicked him off and told him to run behind. Mum was relieved when I arrived back home with them both. Barbara had nothing for the baby. Mum bought a pram and a baby layette and we collected things from friends.

Frank, of course, got round Mum and she gave him another chance, letting him stay with us. I was at work, Jacky was at school and Barbara helped Mum. I came in from work and caught Frank hitting Barbara. I grabbed him, telling him he was a coward and told him to pick which window pane he wanted to go through. I don't agree with men hitting women, full stop.

One evening we were playing cards in the living room round the table. We were all drawn to the cellar door because the knob on the door was turning on its own. Without thinking I said, "It must be Dad coming back to see us." Everyone ran out of the front door and stood outside the house; I was left sitting at the table on my own. I shouted that I was only joking. Mum said, "Will you check that no one is in the cellar and that the chains are secure?" I unlocked the cellar door. There was no light in the cellar so I had to go down with a torch. There were two rooms in the cellar and as I went into the room where we kept the coal, to check that the grate from the road was secure, I felt something touch my shoulder. My heart missed a beat and I think I shouted out in shock. Mum shouted, "What's wrong?"

I said, "Nothing, I'm checking the grate." It was all secure. Coming back out I caught something on my shoulder again. I shone the torch - there was a chain hanging on a nail on the wall, so I knew it wasn't Dad that had touched me. I went up the steps, relocked the cellar door and told Mum everything was safe. I must say it was a bit scary.

Frank and Barbara found accommodation on Park Avenue, Mansfield. Mum was in hospital. Jacky and I had always been close. One day her friends got her a bit tipsy, I don't know where they got the drink. I was being a bit over-protective with her and I took two of her friends home. This caused a fall out with Jacky and she was angry with me. Mum came out of hospital. She said, "You know I'm dying and you've not got the guts to tell me the truth." Jacky wasn't talking to me, I was going to work, doing the housework, trying to look after Mum and every time I came in from work Mum would keep on at me, saying, "Why can't you just tell me the truth?"

I didn't know which way to turn. My husband, Barry, was lying, saying he was going to work, and he never did. He would walk round town all day and come home like he'd had a hard day. Then I found out I was having a baby. On the same day Mum went on at me. She was crying and said, "Just tell me the truth, am I going to die with this cancer?" I felt she already knew and wanted confirmation. I just blurted it out, "Yes Mum, now you've got the truth." The minute I said it I wanted to bite my tongue off. I knew I had to leave though I didn't want to. I knew Mum hadn't got long left to live. I just had to go, I really couldn't face watching my mum suffer anymore. We packed and left Mum's. Nita, my friend, lived in Woodhouse and still had her stables. Her mum gave Barry and me a home in their large house and smallholding; the house was near Albert Square. I hadn't been to my doctor's as I had put off going with everything else that was happening in my life. Barry as usual never got a job, so I was earning the money to keep us.

Two months after I had left home I got a message that Mum was very close to the end of her life. I went up home to see her. Aunty Helen told me my mum didn't want to see me and she tried to stop me going in. Aunty Gladys let me in and took me up to see my mum. My grandma was sat with her and Mum was nearly too ill to speak, but she said "You've got your wish." I could have dropped on the spot. No matter what we had gone through, I would never wish my mum dead. My grandmother told me to say something. I couldn't, I was speechless. I went back to Nita's absolutely heartbroken. That night my mum passed away.

I found out the day of her funeral from Aunty Gladys. Aunty Helen told me I wouldn't be allowed to go but I went - no one was going to stop me. I was feeling for Jacky and not allowed to talk to her, not even at the funeral. I finally went to my doctor and found out I was 7 months pregnant. I was given a midwife, Cynthia, from Woodhouse. She came to visit me and looked after me. I trusted Cynthia and booked a home birth. Barry's grandma and granddad came to fetch me; they wanted me to live with them and for me to have my baby at their house. Barry had been born there, at 8 Bold Street off Chesterfield Road. I was told that I couldn't have Cynthia at that address - it was out of her area. Barry's mum and dad lived on Dorothy Avenue, off Woodhouse Road. They told me I could have my baby at their house so that I could keep Cynthia as my midwife and still have a home delivery.

On December 4th, at 1.50am, I was walking down Chesterfield Road after waking up with labour pains. I had no money to get a taxi. My waters had broken and Barry panicked. I said to him, "I'm going to cut over the Sherwood pit lane." When I walked into Barry's mum's back door my waters broke again. Barry's mum was panicking. She said, "Should I call Cynthia?"
I said, "Not yet, make a cup of tea." I was timing my pains. It got to 7am and I told Barry's mum she could call Cynthia. She arrived at 8am. She said to me, "You are so calm, Mary!" I told her I was going for a bath. She asked me if I wanted her to go with me but I told her to have a cup of tea, I would be alright. At 9.45am I went up to the bedroom and at 10am Cynthia delivered my son. He weighed in at 6lbs 8oz. My baby had been born a month early. I wanted to name him "Paul Mark" but when Barry went to register him he forgot to add on "Mark".

Barry's mum and dad wanted us to stay with them till we got a place of our own, so we were now living with them. Barry, as usual, failed to get a job. His dad was sad that his son was such a disappointment to him.

In a period of just over three years I had lost both my parents under tragic circumstances and married a man who was totally unreliable and bone idle - a man I married for the wrong reason.

My mum is on the left with her friend while she was

battling cancer (taken 1961)

# CHAPTER 7

# A FAILING MARRIAGE

Paul, my son, was my life: I lived for him. Barry's dad got Barry a job at Welbeck pit and we were given a pit house: 1 Longden Terrace, Warsop. I was going out to work in the fields, potato picking, pea picking, etc. to make ends meet, but Barry was letting his dad down by not going into work. I was packing his snap box and giving him his bus fares but he was going into Mansfield, walking round all day, then coming home saying that he had been to work. He made up excuse after excuse for not bringing home any wages. He made us homeless. Fortunately I managed to rent a bungalow on Manvers Street, still in Warsop. Paul was nine months old when I found out I was expecting again. I couldn't get a full time job as Barry refused to look after Paul while I went to work. I couldn't get any help unless I was willing to let Barry go to prison for failing to support us financially. I felt in a no-win situation. Barry was meeting other women behind my back and committing adultery. He was physically and mentally abusing me. His mother was supporting him behind his dad's back.

On June 26th, 1964, I gave birth to my daughter, Lynn, at 3.00 in the morning. The midwife thought I was going to lose my baby. It was a hard labour - Lynn was a breach baby and only weighed 5lbs 2oz. That morning, six hours after I gave birth, the gas man called to read the meter. It had been broken into and the money was gone. I knew that only Barry could have done this. I begged the gas man to wait while I went down to the Post Office to collect Paul's family allowance so that I could pay the bill. He could see the stress I was under and that I had just had my baby. He waited and I ran down to the Post Office, collected my money, came back and paid him. He put a new seal on the meter and let it go for my sake. He was going out the door just as the midwife was coming in. The midwife lived in Warsop on Sherwood Street. She had seen me running down the street and she really told me off. She called me a foolhardy girl and asked me if I was trying to kill myself. I broke down and had to tell her the truth in confidence. She told me I would be better off without Barry. I knew she was right. He got on his knees and begged me to give him another chance. I tried to think what the right thing to do for my children was. Then Barry's grandma passed away and Barry's mum moved into her house.

Thanks to Barry we were soon homeless again. I didn't know what to do: I had two young children and we were on the street. I can remember standing at the bottom of

Belvedere Street with my two young children and a pram, just sobbing. Barry had run off and left me. I only had enough money to get the children a warm drink. We had no change of clothing, only what we were wearing. I walked through the streets of Mansfield and went on to Titchfield Park. There was a shelter on the park with a bench. I spent the night in the shelter. I had wrapped Paul and Lynn in the pram blankets and my coat; I was very cold. In the early morning I walked up to 8 Bold Street, back to Barry's mum and dad's. They took me and the children in. Lynn had caught a bad cold. I told Barry's dad I was going to find work to keep my children and that I would pay for a nursery to care for them while I was working. Cherokee Nursery took both my children for the price of one. I went to work at Pleasley Mills. On my second day at work the nursery rang to tell me Lynn was very poorly with a high temperature and they brought her home. I took her straight to hospital and was told she had pneumonia. I thought I was going to lose her. Barry came to the hospital but soon left: he didn't want to know. I stayed at the hospital with her overnight and Barry's mum stayed with her while I went to work. Thank God my little girl survived.

We stayed with Barry's mum and dad for quite a while and they took Barry back in. He did nothing to help and his mum charged me for his keep. I was going to work, cooking all the meals and helping with the housework.

The house was overcrowded and I felt I had no privacy with my children. Barry's mum and dad started to fall out. It wasn't nice: they just didn't speak to each other and kept passing messages by whoever was available. I felt as if me and my children were a burden. I went down to the Council and spoke to Mrs Betts. She was lovely: she found me a property on Portland Street and met me there. It had been a fish shop and wanted a lot of decorating. I got the keys on the Friday, bought paint and wallpaper and did both the bedrooms and landing over the weekend. Mrs Betts came on the Monday - she was amazed at what I had done. She gave me two weeks rent free so that I could finish most of the work.

We moved in. I managed to earn enough money to buy some second-hand furniture and I was given some bedding and towels by friends. I wasn't in long when Barry arrived with a young girl. I went to the shop to get some milk. When I returned this young girl told me Barry had tried to interfere with her. That was the last straw. I went to the girl's parents and told them to prosecute him but they let him get away with it. He went out and I was sat with a box of tablets, feeling desperate. I was going to take them but John, a young teenager who had come to visit, stopped me. He threw my tablets on the fire. Then Janet, one of the friends I had worked with on the buses before I married Barry, came to see me. She told me I looked a mess and she was taking me home with her. She had appreciated that I had helped her out when she was homeless a few years before. She gave me and my children a home. In return I worked for her, helping her run her home for homeless young people on Beech Avenue, off Nottingham Road.

Even if I had wanted to go back to my home I couldn't. Barry had given the family that declined to prosecute him everything out of the house. We had no home to go back to. Janet had eight youngsters from broken homes when she took us in in 1966. Paul was four years old and Lynn was two and a half. Janet taught me all she could: she was my teacher and mentor. We worked together with some of the most vulnerable homeless young people who needed a secure and safe home. They were young people who had suffered some very traumatic and unsettled lives.

Janet was watching Lynn one day. She walked behind Lynn with a tray and dropped the tray behind her. It made such a clatter but Lynn didn't look up, she just carried on drawing. "Just as I thought, Mary, we must get Lynn's hearing checked, I think she's deaf." I took Lynn to have her ears checked. The GP sent her to be tested at the hospital on a machine. They confirmed that my daughter was deaf with what they called "glue ear". Lynn was now four and the hospital said they could not operate on her until she reached the age of five. I realised that Lynn had taught herself to lip read. She started school at King Edward's, off Littleworth. She had to have her ears operated on and she came back home with grommets in her ears to drain away the fluid. Lynn had lost a lot of school time and was behind the other children.

Janet and I were working with the probation office, police, courts, social services, hospitals, doctors, schools and councils. We also worked with personnel officers in factories and firms to help our young people find work. Mrs Price from Illingworths rang me to see if I could go to the Sutton factory, saying she would like a word with me. She made me a cup of tea and we had a chat about the young people she had employed for us. She was more than pleased with them and was prepared to give more employment to any of our residents in the future.

I met some wonderful people and I want to name some of them: Miss Kelly, the almoner of Mansfield Hospital; Miss Seager of the probation service; Mr Clark, social security manager; Mr Dodds, Mansfield and Sutton Health Department; Mr Hughes, Head of Social Services; Mr Hinds, Head of Housing; and Mrs Betts, housing allocation officer at St John Street. All these people were professionals who went above and beyond the call of duty. Mansfield should be very proud of them. I am very proud of all the young people who went through our hands - they rose above their backgrounds. Most moved on and became hard working, successful and decent citizens within the community.

In 1968 we went to look at a large house on Chesterfield Road - Janet was thinking of expanding her service. We had just passed West Notts College when Janet tripped and fell, hurting her shoulder. It shook her up so I took her back home. The next day she was in agony with her shoulder - she thought she might have dislocated it. I rang my Uncle Wilf who worked as an osteopath. He also had a herbal shop along with his surgery in the Handley Arcade. I asked him if he could call in and check out Janet's shoulder. He told Janet her shoulder was not dislocated and advised her to go for an x-ray. I went to the hospital with her. She was sent for some x-rays and blood tests. One of the doctors then wanted to speak with me. He told me that Janet had got cancer, and that it had already spread right through her body and she was on borrowed time.

I nursed Janet right to the end. She asked me to make her two promises: that I would bring her son up as my own until he became independent, and that I would continue to fight for the cause of homelessness. I kept both those promises. On the morning Janet was losing her battle to live, Father Hatter from St Mark's Church came round and stayed to give me support until Janet passed away. There was no way I could ever repay her kindness and compassion, or the support she gave to everyone she took under her wing, sharing herself equally among the many. She taught me to be caring of others' needs, to be patient and understanding, to be compassionate and non-judgmental. It was yet another tragic loss of a very dear friend. Andrew, her son, was too young to deal with the funeral, and I couldn't find her sister. I dealt with the funeral and laid Janet to rest in Mansfield Cemetery on Nottingham Road.

I was now 31 years of age, with 18 young people and 3 children to bring up - Andrew, Paul and Lynn. Social Services asked Andrew if he wanted to go into care. There was no way this was going to happen. Andrew told them himself that he was staying with me and that he would run straight back to me if they tried to take him. I now knew that my life had been planned out for me.

# CHAPTER 8

# HOMELESSNESS IS NOW MY CAUSE

I didn't have time to grieve over losing Janet, there was so much to sort out. The most important task was to secure the home for the young people. The property leased out to Janet had been obtained for her by Miss Seeger, a Senior Probation Officer. I made an appointment with Mr Macdonald at Mansfield District Council's finance office on Albert Street. I explained that Janet had passed away and asked him if there was any chance of me taking on the lease to continue with her work. He commented that my face was familiar and asked me my maiden name. When I told him he asked if my dad was named "Frank". I confirmed that he was. Mr Macdonald then told me that if I was half the worker my dad was then he was willing to trust me. He turned the lease over to me and told me not to let him down. He even said he would find me a larger, better property if he could. That was it, there was no way I had any intention of letting him down. I worked hard and all the services were supporting me.

A neighbour, Mrs Hurt, came over and invited me to her house for a cup of tea. She commented that it took a special person to work all the hours I was working. I told her of my promise to Janet. She told me she was the secretary of the local Labour Party and that she would give me all the support I needed. She asked me to become a member of the Labour Party and took me to the Labour club near the Victoria pub on Albert Street. I got to know some of the local councillors: Mr Williams, Mr and Mrs Gallagher, Mr Bygroves, and Mr Groves, a county councillor. The local MP was Mr Concanon. My brother-in-law, Mr Naylor, became a member of the Labour Party at the same time. He was very dedicated and loyal to the people of Mansfield. He went to Ruskin College to study politics, later becoming a councillor. But I was too busy to get involved in politics. Mrs Hurt used to hold council meetings, laying on food and drinks at her house. I was always invited to attend. I remember meeting Alan Meale, who later became the Mansfield MP, at some of these gatherings. (He was later knighted in the Queen's Birthday Honours list in 2011 and is now Sir Alan Meale). He was also very supportive in my cause to get more accommodation for the homeless. Mrs Hurt encouraged me to join Toc-H, a church charity founded by Tubby Clayton around 1915 to support ex-servicemen in the memory of a soldier who died, Gilbert Talbot. I believe he also founded a voluntary institution, a Christian youth centre, in 1920.The badge was a small lamp, with the meaning, "where there is a small flicker of light, there is hope". We used to have meetings in St Peter's church house at the bottom of Midworth Street.

Back at home some residents were moving on to independence. As they moved on, another young person was waiting to move in. New probation officers, new social workers - all were becoming a part of my life. I had a book for registering my residents and books for all my incomings, outgoings, expenses etc. I did my books on a weekly basis so that if anyone wanted to check them everything was above board and legal. I was only charging £5.50 per week full board, the same as Janet had previously set. Other landladies were charging £10.00 board - they did it for a living. I kept my young people's rent low so that if they got a job they had money in their pockets: this gave them an incentive to find work.

I was living on a shoe string, budgeting all the time. I thought it was important to find things to keep my young people occupied. I had a dart board, board games, packs of playing cards, dominoes, jigsaw puzzles and a one-armed bandit machine. On Wednesdays I would move the furniture back so that they could wrestle for fun. I was quite happy to join in with them. Friday nights were dance nights, it was on with the records, on with the music. It saved them going out spending money in the local pubs. It was my job to keep them out of trouble. On some Sundays I would organise a treasure hunt. I would go on to Titchfield Park, hide small amounts of money under stones, near trees, or in other places that made it a challenge for them. It was great fun. I would give them some clues. I used to encourage them to keep their bedrooms clean by rewarding them with little treats. I didn't mind them inviting one of their friends for dinner. I used to make meals that would go round: shepherd's pie, meat and potato pies, stew and dumplings. On Sundays we always had roast beef and Yorkshire puddings with veg, peas and gravy, or roast chicken and stuffing. All meals and desserts were homemade to keep costs down. I used to make all my own pastry, cakes and trifles.

I had some real characters. They kept me busy and they played a lot of jokes. I had a new resident and some of the lads started talking about ghosts. I knew something was being planned. The lad said he didn't believe in ghosts and wasn't scared of anything. Janice, one of my girls, went into town the next day and bought some illuminating paint. When everybody had gone to bed Janice put the paint on her hands and face, put a white sheet over her clothes, turned out the lights and came into my room. All I could see were the bones in her hands and face like a skeleton, it was very effective. She crept into the boys' room in the dark, making a ghostly noise, and then she ran back into the girls' room. The boy left the next day and I never saw him again. On another occasion, I was talking to a social worker in the hallway at the bottom of the stairs. I felt drops of water on my head; the social worker must have felt them, too. She kept looking up but didn't say anything. I looked up and just saw Janice ducking down on the landing. After the social worker left I ran upstairs and caught Janice; the next thing we were in the hall, wrestling on the floor. I sat on Janice and asked one of the residents to fetch me a bowl of water. I was pouring it onto Janice but she knocked the bowl of water away. We were wrestling and rolling around the hallway, getting wet through and roaring with laughter. Then we had to clear up the mess. I must admit it was fun. On another occasion some of the lads made a ghost out of a mop and wrapped a sheet around it. Everyone had gone to bed. I came out of my room to go to the bathroom and walked into the sheet. They had secured it to the ceiling outside my bedroom, hoping to hear me scream. I just pushed it out of the way. I had to smile: that one didn't work!

I came down to do breakfast one morning, unlocked the door and saw a mess of mud leading from one of my neighbour's gardens. I went out and swept it up - I didn't want any mud brought into the house. The police called to say that Mr Sooby had reported that all his potatoes had been dug up overnight and could they talk to my boys? They said they were taking them to the station to question them. They took all 14 of my lads. I had cooked the dinners thinking they might be back but the police told me they were going to keep them in the cells overnight. I asked them if I could take the lads' dinners down - I didn't want to throw away 14 dinners. I was given permission to take them down, so I walked up the street into the police station with a pram. It was the only way I could transport the food to the police station. The dinners were in containers and the plates were separate. I had to plate them up at the police station. After all that the police only charged two of the lads: they'd done it for a dare.

Everything was moving too fast for me. Mr Ainsworth, a solicitor, rang me from court asking me to go down straight away - he would explain when I got there. He asked me if I could find a bed for a young man who had committed a minor crime and was homeless. If he couldn't find accommodation or someone to vouch for this young man he would be sent to prison. I was called to the bench in front of the magistrate. He asked me if I was willing to give the young man a chance and accommodation. I agreed and he placed him into my care.

The magistrate was my neighbour, Mr Sooby. I got a shock when a Rolls Royce Silver Cloud pulled up outside my front door and I saw Mr Sooby coming to see me. He thanked me and told me that he had heard of all the hard work I was doing for the homeless in Mansfield. He said if there was anything he could do to help me he would. He asked me if I was short of beds or furniture. He told me he was an auctioneer and invited me to his auction rooms on Dame Flogan Street. He also told me to put my hand up in the auction room when I saw something I could use. Mr Sooby became a good friend and gave me support, help and advice. He was a partner in Sooby, Crompton and Eastgate estate agents and a very distinguished man.

During this time I had a message to say that Aunty Nell, my dad's sister, wanted me to go up to see her. One of my residents, Jim, had bought a Lambretta, an ex-army scooter. It was large and heavy. He had bought it to ride to and from work. He worked in the Hide and Skin factory on Midworth Street. I had helped him learn to ride it. I asked him if I could borrow his scooter to go up to my aunty's. He lent me the bike and off I went. I had no problems on the way there, the bike was running fine. My aunty wanted me to know her husband, Uncle Bill, was suffering with his health. On the way back home I slowed at the bottom of Newgate Lane, outside the King's Arms pub. On pulling out onto the main road my gears bit too quickly and the scooter shot off with me, out of control. I was mounting the pavement and going to hit a brick wall. I couldn't pull the scooter straight, it was too heavy. So I had to pull it down on top of me. The seat shot up and petrol was coming out of the tank. I pulled the scooter back up and jammed the seat down to stop the petrol from running out. I was injured and some men were watching me from the steps of the King's Arms. I felt so stupid as I walked home pushing the scooter. As I was coming through Titchfield Park Andy took it off me and pushed it home. There was a big dent in the frame. I told Jim I'd get it repaired. The next day I saw John Hallam, who lived on Duke Street, repairing his motorbike and he agreed to look at the scooter. When I went to collect it he had done a perfect job of getting out the dent. I wanted to pay him but he wouldn't accept any money. I said, "You can't work for nothing," but he told me he appreciated the work I did for the young people in my care. John and his sister, Jacky, have been my friends for many years now.

I was busy serving dinners one day when a reporter from the Evening Post called at the door. He told me I had been nominated for a free holiday in Italy for my hard work and commitment to the homeless people of Mansfield. I had been chosen out of the nominations sent forward by the public. I thought it was someone playing a joke. I told the reporter to call back when I wasn't so busy. He came back the next day with the holiday information and flight tickets. He took some photos of me with my residents. I only had one week to sort out someone to look after everything for me, and for someone to look after my children. Barbara, a probation officer who had become a good friend, told me not to worry - she would look after my children, Paul and Lynn, at her home until I got back off the holiday. Andy wanted to stay at home with the residents. I went into the town and saw the placards saying: "Guardian Angel Flying To The Sun". Printed in the Nottingham Evening Post was a story of all the work I did to keep the homeless people of Mansfield off the streets. I felt rather overwhelmed by all the publicity. The holiday was absolutely amazing. The son of the Hyde Barker Travel Agency took me to Luton Airport. I made some friends on the tour. We visited Sorrento, Naples, Capri, Rome etc. Barbara had been fantastic to take care of my children for me.

Ted Perry was another Probation Officer who supported the young people in finding them accommodation to keep them safe and off the streets. John and Hilda Eddershaw were also Probation Officers who became my friends. There were also two police officers who helped and supported my young people on many occasions: DC Ken Gibson and his wife Christine. Ken was promoted to the drugs squad in Nottingham and Christine became Head of the Sherwood Lodge Police HQ in Arnold.

After that holiday I met David, my future husband - much more about him later!

My friend Christine had turned up homeless with her baby son. I called him Reggae after the record Johnny Reggae (by The Piglets) in 1971. I loved my work: I was totally committed and dedicated to my residents. I intended to keep fighting for the plight of the homeless, and fight I did. I fought to get some hostels opened in Mansfield. All my residents were registered with my own GP practice, Roundwood Surgery on Wood Street (Dr Harrison, Dr Golshetti, Dr Ovary, Dr Steiner, and Dr Burns). All the doctors supported me and I knew that I could call them at any time. I have been given an updated report by Dr Tadpatrica that the Roundwood Surgery was rated as one the best 20 in the country by the Care Quality Commission.

I had taken the residents on a picnic up to the park at the bottom of Berry Hill Road. Steven and his sister were wrestling on the grass and, somehow, Lynn got tossed up in the air. When she landed I ran to her. I noticed a large swelling at the top of her thigh and phoned for a taxi to get her to the hospital quickly. I told the doctor I thought she had injured her hip. He agreed with me and they had to operate on her quickly. She had dislocated her hip. She was put in plaster, then on to traction to level her hips. Had I not acted so quickly, Lynn would have had to wear a built-up shoe. I took up all her school work to do while she was in the hospital so that she didn't get behind. I had to take her to school in a wheelchair after she came home from hospital: she was still in plaster. Paul then had an accident - he was pushed off a wall and blood was coming out of his ear. I took him straight to the hospital thinking he might have burst his eardrum. The doctor told me that Paul had a fracture at the base of his skull, and the blood coming out of his ear helped to release the pressure. Paul was OK and allowed home.

Mr Dobbs, the Mental Health Officer for the local Health Authority, called. He brought me a new resident, little Jean. She had disabilities and worked at the Remploy off Sutton Road. She was so quiet when she first arrived. She would stand in the hallway holding her handbag, she would go into the dining room for her dinner and not say a word, eat her dinner, and then return to the hall until she went to bed. I waited for Jean to come to me in her own time. After a few weeks she came to me and told me she couldn't get any more money into her handbag. She had been paying me her board out of her wages, and just putting the rest into her handbag. She asked me if I could save it for her. I told her it would be better to put it in the bank. She had not got a bank account so I took her to the main post office on Church St and helped her open a savings account. I told her that when she got her wages she should put the money into her account before coming home. Now I understood why she always kept hold of her handbag. The change in little Jean was amazing, she even joined in the dancing on Friday nights.

Sue, another of my residents, had epilepsy. She swallowed her tongue once and I had to bring her tongue back; I had to act quickly to stop her choking. Mr Dobbs brought me another resident - another little lady, we called her little Janet. She kept sending for an ambulance, wasting their time: she just wanted attention. I gave her a job helping me in the kitchen. She became my little helper and she loved it because she could put the kettle on for a cuppa. Visitors were always dropping in. It was common knowledge among the residents that, when someone new came and had settled in, they got christened. They would half fill the bath with tepid water, grab the new resident, carry them to the bathroom and put them fully clothed into the bath.

I never gave up fighting to get a hostel opened in Mansfield. Christine said I should go out more, I wasn't getting a social life. She took me to the Little Midlands pub on Belvedere Street - they had "free and easy" nights. Rosie played the piano and the customers used to get up and sing a song. My future husband, David, was a painter and decorator by trade. I could only go out socially once a week on Saturday night. We met some wonderful people who were very talented. David was a singer - a jazz and blues man. He used to sing "Birth of the Blues", "Mac the Knife", "Jessabell", "Georgia", "Frankie and Johnny" etc. He had sung for many years with Rosie: she used to play the piano in the Blue Boar in the town centre when David would come on leave from the army in the Second World War. Rosie knew David's every move when he was up singing. Max was another singer. He used to sing "Help Me Make It Through The Night" by Gladys Knight. He had long hair and a hang-dog expression. Max and I used to sing a duet: "There's a hole in my bucket dear Liza". For charity the landlord used to go round the pub with a bucket while we were singing for customers to drop their change in. There are some very happy memories there.

At Christmas, 1973, Lynn came up with Linda, one of my residents' daughters. Lynn was nine years of age at the time. They loved Rosie. She used to drop in with us for a cup of tea and sometimes a meal. The girls sang "Paper Roses" as a treat for Rosie. The customers and friends passed round a hat and collected for the girls. Lynn and Linda shared the money with Linda's younger sister, Betty, a beautiful little girl who had a heart defect.

One day Sue took ill and was rushed into hospital. My neighbour, Margaret Bantam, went along in the ambulance with Sue and me. It was late so the hospital wouldn't let us go on to the ward with Sue as they didn't want us to disturb sleeping patients. They told us to go up next day. That night I went to bed and had a strange dream - or at least I thought it was a dream. Janet came back to me and told me to go with her through the window. I left my body and went with her. She took me to see Sue who was in a corner of the ward with a window at the side. Janet took me through the window and we sat on the bench below, talking. She told me to look after Sue and to protect her. She felt Sue had already suffered too much before coming to us. I then woke up. On the way to the hospital I told Margaret about my dream. When we got on to the ward we were stunned to find that Sue's bed was in the corner with a window beside it. Margaret looked through the window and said, "That was no dream, Mary. The bench you mentioned is here below the window." I believe that Janet did indeed come back and take me to see Sue in hospital, and that I had an out of body experience.

A new year and what a year! The district councillors all came to the home. We had big discussions on what was needed to help the plight of the homeless. I let them check through my books. They were amazed how I had managed to look after so many without having asked or received any funding. Councillor Jim Hawkins became a supporter and a friend. David explained how homelessness was increasing and escalating. All of them agreed that the Council should help. With support from all the services, the Council and many good people I was able to help some of the most vulnerable young people of Mansfield and surrounding areas.

I was still attending court in support of the young homeless people in my care. I was meeting solicitors: Mr Aspley, Mr Bacon, and Mr Ainsworth. Mr Bacon was a young solicitor who would fight for the rights of young offenders under the Legal Aid system. He was one of the most amazing to watch in court - I put him on a par with Perry Mason! I admired Mr Aspley, with his many years of experience and as a gentleman who would always acknowledge me in the courtroom. Mr Ainsworth became my solicitor and a very good friend.

In 1974 Mr Hind, the Leader of the Council, rang me from his office at the Manor House in Woodhouse. He asked me to go down as soon as possible, saying he had some good news for me. He greeted me at the main entrance and escorted me through to his office. He told me that the Council had found me a large house that had previously been an old people's home: "Sunnycroft" in The Park, off Park Avenue, Mansfield. He drove me there in his car to show me the property and the grounds.

I accepted the property! I couldn't wait to tell the residents and my children. In 1974 we moved into Sunnycroft. I was a little sad to be leaving Beech Avenue, but looking forward to a new challenge.

Enjoying the holiday I was nominated for by the public for my work with the homeless.

Me – In Sorrento, Italy in 1973

# CHAPTER 9

# SUNNYCROFT

When Mr Hind took me to see Sunnycroft I couldn't believe I was being given the keys to this beautiful property, all in its own grounds. This usually only happens in dreams. The house was a three storey building and Mr Hind told me that it had previously been a residential care home for up to 30 elderly and disabled residents. It had to be closed down as a residential home as it would cost too much to bring it up to the Medical Board's standard. It was only in need of redecorating, minor repairs and tidying up the grounds. At the back of the house were gardens, lawns and a large pool with a fountain. At the side near to the entrance were gardens, an orchard with apple and pear trees, and stables at the bottom. Besides offering bed spaces for 28 residents, plus my family, it gave us a spacious car park, a snooker room, a substantial kitchen and dining room, as well as attractive features such as an impressive bay window on the first floor. Although not offering much more accommodation (there were already 26 residents at Beech Avenue) there was so much more space, inside and out!

After viewing all this I was completely overwhelmed. Mr Hind gave me the keys, and said, "It's all yours now, Mary." The Council left it all furnished - all the beds and bedding, the snooker table, and a coal house full of coal. I couldn't get home quick enough to tell everybody. After dinner I went to find David to give him my good news. He was still living in Rainworth, in lodgings, with his friends Sheila and Dennis. I knew he would be in The Ram, playing cards with some of his other friends. I went into The Ram and told him I wanted to tell him something. He packed in his hand and came outside with me. I told him that I had been given the keys to a property on Park Avenue. I didn't want to tell him about the house - I wanted to see his face when I took him to view it. He was absolutely stuck for words. After seeing the property he asked how soon I could move in. I told him Mr Hinds had left that decision up to me. David said he would start the decorating straight away. He put in for his holidays at work. He was working for a firm in Woodhouse respraying and painting caravans for a businessman, Mr D. Haggerty, and his wife Claire. They let David have the time off to help me.

Before my residents and family moved in David had painted the kitchen, the dining room and some of the residents' bedrooms. While David was doing the decorating I was cleaning and bleaching the toilets, bathrooms, sinks and cookers, and making my way to the launderette at Woodhouse to do all the bedding, towels and tea towels. I had to use the washers and driers and I can't begin to tell you the hours I spent there. I wanted to make all the beds up with clean bedding before moving the residents in. Then I had to wash all the cubicle curtains. It was a mammoth task as I was also helping the residents to prepare everything for the move. We were both working 24/7. I had decided to let David move in with us, giving him a cubicle in the annexe with two older residents, Fred and Arthur. I had applied to get a divorce from my husband, Barry, and was waiting for my case to come up in the Divorce Court.

Jim Hinchcliffe, who worked for the Chad, went round Mansfield streets with David and me, taking and handing out drinks, sandwiches and cigarettes and talking to homeless people who were sleeping rough in a derelict cafe at the bottom of Belvedere Street and in empty, broken-down houses at the end of Bancroft Lane. "Uncle Jim", as he was known, took photographs and wrote a story in the Chad about the plight of these unfortunate, vulnerable people, proving to us that other people cared. The police also helped to make this possible: they wanted to get homeless people off the streets. Our fight was to continue to house homeless families and women fleeing violence. We needed all the services working together and this was starting to happen. Sunnycroft was the first step. The Council then opened Oakdene on Crow Hill

Drive as a safe house for women and children fleeing violence.

Back at Sunnycroft David was becoming an important part of my life. He gave up his job as a decorator to help me out, though I was too busy to think about a relationship at this point. Homelessness had now become a challenge for him, too. We were working together as a team. David was doing all the decorating, shopping and maintenance; I was doing all the baking, meals, cooking, cleaning and washing. David would advise and help the boys; I was there for the girls. We were now taking in residents aged from the cradle to the grave: single, elderly, and homeless families. There were people turning up on the doorstep that we couldn't help. We were full to the rafters, and yet people never gave up trying to join us. The residents were not moving on, they were happy to stay.

In the first year at Sunnycroft, we had done so much work. The Probation Office sent us a team of young people who were on the community work programme and being trained to become gardeners, to help us out. They were supervised by Mr B Gutteridge and they worked hard, weeding, digging and planting. They drained and cleaned out the pool. They helped us to bring the gardens and the grounds up to a very high standard. We could not thank Mr Gutteridge and the boys enough - they did us proud. The greenhouse was flourishing and providing us with fresh tomatoes, cucumbers, lettuce, and mushrooms. In the orchard we grew apples and pears. We had a donkey named Vulcan and a horse called Darkie in the field at the side of the house. The hall and staircase were wall to wall carpeted and we put up new curtains to all the windows. David painted all the front of the house. The only way he could finish the job was to strap a paint brush to a bush stale so that he could reach to the top of the building. We put on garden parties to help raise funds for St Peter's Church, Toc H and local charities.

The bread and milk were delivered every morning. David cooked all the breakfasts. He would open the kitchen window so that everybody could smell the bacon cooking. He would make bacon sandwiches and cups of tea for the milkman, baker and postman. The residents used to let the elderly get their breakfast first, then everyone else would follow. The dining room tables would be all set and ready before mealtimes. Dr Harrison used to walk into the kitchen, smell the dinner being cooked and jokingly say, "Have you got one to spare?" He always found the time to have a chat and a cup of tea with us. Mr Hind from the Council used to bring round the councillors. He was pleased to escort them round Sunnycroft. We allowed visitors to look round our home and we made everyone welcome. We set up the dining room with a little hot water boiler, a tea urn, milk jugs, sugar basins, coffee percolator, cups, saucers and plates, so if a large party of people came to look round they could help themselves to drinks. It helped out a lot, especially at our garden parties. We were proud of Sunnycroft and proud of what we had achieved, and especially proud of our residents. They would all chip in together if we were busy and they would always be polite to our visitors. Janet helped in the kitchen, Sue did all the washing for me, and Steve helped me with the horses and gardening. We had a pianola given to us by an elderly neighbour. Jack, who was nicknamed Romper, used to play the piano. The pianola scrolls played just by using the pedals. Jack had a little job playing the piano at The Bull, down Woodhouse Road.

David asked me to marry him, but I couldn't at that time: I had to get my divorce from Barry. I had known David for five years. How many men would have waited that long for someone? He was a man who had saved me from having a breakdown in 1970. A man who had been there for me and my children, who had fought with me for the plight of the homeless, who I knew truly loved me and was my soulmate. I only wish I had been free to marry David earlier. My strict upbringing gave me strong morals. My husband had been cheating on me for years. His dad came to see me - he told me how proud of me he was. He said he would always come to see me while he could. He met David and advised me to get a divorce from his son, admitting I would be so much better off without him.

Barry's dad passed away shortly after. Barry had moved in with my cousin who lived on Ravensdale Road. I was going to follow Barry's dad at his funeral. His mum rang me to ask me to walk with Barry for appearance's sake. I couldn't. I felt this time she had asked too much but I did send a wreath out of respect from me, Barry and the children. I went to the hairdresser's on the day of the funeral and put on a new dress. David told me I looked beautiful. I went into the bathroom just before the time of the funeral and washed my hair out. David asked me what I was doing. I said, "Something I should have done years ago. I'm washing Barry out of my hair and out of my life."

David replied, "Does that mean I've got a chance then?" I told him yes. David deserved a chance: we became partners in work and partners in life. The song sung by Anne Murray, "You Needed Me", says it all. David had picked me up when I was down, he gave me the strength to face the world out on my own again, and he always put me on a pedestal. I realised we had built a life together and we needed each other. I hadn't really stopped to think about my own life and what I wanted. I realised that I had learnt to trust David. I knew I could depend on him. He was already a big part of my life and my children loved him. Paul was now 14, Lynn 12 and Andy 20. My sister, Jacky, and her husband, Graham, had two lovely boys, Gavin, who was born on Christmas Day, 1969 and Paul, born 28th June, 1971. Gavin was now 7 and Paul 5.

That year I rediscovered my brother Fred, who I had been trying to find for a long time. He only lived in Warsop. David helped me to find him and took me to his house. I knocked on the door not knowing how my brother and his family would feel. My sister-in-law, Dorothy, answered the door. She recognised me and told me they had heard I was looking for Fred, and that I looked like him. Fred was the double of my dad. He put his arms around me and gave me a big hug saying he had been waiting for me to come. Janet, my niece, was playing on the floor and my two nephews John and David were at work. It didn't take long for us all to unite as a completed family. I met Fred's mum. I called her Aunty Connie out of respect; she was lovely and made me welcome. She said to me, "Now you've found him, promise me you will never let him go." I kept that promise. Jacky was also pleased that I had found our brother: the three of us were so much alike. I took Fred and Dorothy up to meet our Uncle Cyril, my dad's brother. Uncle Cyril was so pleased that we had found our brother. Fred was a lovely man with a lovely family, a good father and husband, a hard working man. He worked at Glaspell drift mine then later moved to Warsop Main. Dorothy, Jacky and I have always got on well.

I hope by now you will be realising what an extraordinary, amazing and rewarding life I have led. The good news came that I had won my divorce case on the grounds of adultery. In six weeks' time I would be free to marry David. We could make all the arrangements for our wedding. We had been living together for the past seven months and I was sure I was expecting David's baby, but I needed to get it confirmed. We arranged our Big Day for the 20th of August, 1976, at the registry office on St John Street. Father Hatter of St Mark's Church, one of my neighbours when I lived at Beech Avenue, agreed to bless our wedding on Sunday the 21st of August. We chose this as our official wedding day. We had the wedding reception at Sunnycroft with over 200 guests. Fred was on the bar serving drinks. With help I did all the catering for my own wedding before leaving to go to the church. We had lots of entertainment, a karaoke, bingo, music and dancing. David had made a cosy fire in the snooker room. Some of the guests were helping out. All the rooms plus the kitchen were used. Wedding guests and residents were all enjoying the day. The residents did their bit to help us to clean and tidy up after the wedding. My life now felt complete.

Before I continue (it's now our lives) I am sure David would want me to share an overview of his life before we met. David had gone through many trials and tribulations. He had been abandoned by his mum as a baby and brought up by his dad. His dad had to go to work, leaving David to fend for himself most of the time. He was a well-educated man, who had won a scholarship to higher education, and a dedicated athlete. He used to run for the Sutton Harriers in his youth when he was an apprentice painter and decorator. At the age of 17 he won the Brian Mickey Talent Competition at the Granada in Mansfield's town centre for his gift of singing. He didn't get the chance to pursue his ambition to become a jazz and blues singer. When he was 18 his dad collapsed and died of a heart attack on Elm Tree Street, off Ratcliffe Gate. Disillusioned, he joined the army to fight for his country during the Second World War. He fought in Benghazi and Tobruk. He got blown out of a trench when an enemy plane hit the ground. Some of his friends who dived under a tank all died. David's eardrums were badly damaged and he suffered shrapnel wounds.

After the war there were no jobs in decorating. He became a bus driver for the Trent Barton Bus Company. He used to go into Nottingham and surrounding areas, working round the clubs, singing to help him earn some extra money. With no family he had to live in lodgings. He made some friends in Nottingham who were members of a gang that led him into a life of crime and ended up with him going to prison. He openly told me about his life when we first met; he didn't want me to hear it from someone else. I accepted David as my friend. He was working and wanted to put his past behind him. He wanted to make a fresh start and to move on to a new life. I honestly believe it was fate that brought us together. He had been married twice and divorced. He lost his son with epilepsy and had two daughters, Jo and Jane. I am sure that David would give me his blessing to write this overview of his life in my autobiography. He was a man who worked hard, overrode his past and put so much back into our society.

Two months after our wedding, on the 28th of October, I gave birth to my youngest son. I named him David after his dad. Fred and Dorothy bought all baby clothes for a boy and Dorothy had knitted him sets of pods, mittens, hats, matinee jackets, and a beautiful shawl. This is the time when I met Sister Audrey Cook - she was my midwife. She loved coming up to Sunnycroft. She lived just down the road from me, on Park Avenue. We became close friends and are still friends today. Audrey and Nana Cook were always baking. I used to pop in to visit. Like at my home, the kettle was always on. With 28 residents and my family, David and I only had the weekends to spend a night out together. We would go to the Little Midlands where we would meet up with some of our residents who were old enough to come out and join us. We had so much fun with our residents. We became a very large family. I think David was brave for taking on so much responsibility. He never let me, my family, or our residents down. I can remember most of my residents. So many have gone through our hands over the years and we still have a long way to go. When David Junior was born I let him go to the Cherokee Nursery. I didn't want to neglect him, with me and his dad both working full time. The nursery bus used to pick David up at 7.30 in the morning, when we were doing the breakfasts, returning him home at 6.00 in the evening when we were serving the dinners.

We were still fighting to get another home opened for homeless families. The Chad took photographs of us having to turn away homeless families and young mums with children from Grove House in Clipstone - a home that took in young pregnant girls till they had their babies. They were very limited for space and were only allowed to keep the young mums for a short period of time. A church had already been opened for us to have meetings at lunchtimes on Rosemary Street, once a month. The meeting was called the Midweek Break. Doctor Harrison went along to this meeting with me on the day I gave birth to David Junior. I didn't want to miss the meeting and Doctor Harrison wanted to keep his eye on me. I had given birth to David at 2.45am and I was at the meeting with Doctor Harrison by 12.00 for lunch. Everyone who was important turned up at these meetings. It was the first time all the services were together, all as one fighting for the same cause to get another hostel opened in Mansfield. It was successful, and the Council agreed to open Lochbuie, the large coach house across the road from Sunnycroft, to accommodate homeless families. The Council asked David and me if there was any possibility of us running Lochbuie on the same system we were running Sunnycroft. Being realistic, even with staff, we felt it was too much to ask of ourselves. The Council opened Lochbuie making it a warden-controlled hostel. Mansfield District Council now had three hostels to accommodate the homeless of Mansfield and surrounding areas.

Aunty Nell, my dad's sister, moved in with us; she was poorly and I didn't want her to be put into a nursing home. We gave her our bedroom which was the en suite. David and I moved into the double bedroom on the third floor. Eventually my cousins settled her into a flat on Ladybrook Lane. Aunty Peggy and Uncle Wilf, who was the osteopath in the Handley Arcade, asked me if I could look after Aunty Lucy, my grandma's sister-in-law, to give them a break as Aunty Dorothy in Blackpool was ill. I knew about Aunty Dorothy's illness: she had breast cancer. Uncle Clarry and Aunty Dorothy had asked me to keep it a secret. Before I left Beech Avenue they had offered me the hotel and they were going to leave it to me if anything happened to them. I loved them very dearly. I kept their secret, but I couldn't take on the hotel. I could never have deserted Janet. It was fate that my Aunty Dorothy and Janet both suffered cancer, both so ill at the same time. Uncle Clarry wrote me a lovely letter, thanking me for keeping their secret, and letting me know that my Aunty Dorothy had passed away peacefully in his arms the way they had planned it to be.

No news was good news just then. David and I were also looking after Uncle Cyril. We had taken him and one of his friends to Yarmouth just to visit Fred and Dorothy on their holiday. Uncle Cyril took a bad turn on the way home. I was really worried. It felt like everyone I loved was being taken away from me. So, running the home, doing my duty to my family, and having to leave David with the giant's share of the work left me worrying about David. In 1978 Uncle Cyril committed suicide. He hanged himself in his garage. This affected me so badly. It brought back the memory of my dad's death. But I couldn't abandon my residents. I had to find someone who cared about people, like David and myself. I met Liz who was feeding the homeless people of Mansfield in her cafe on Leeming Street, often out of her own pocket - down and outs who were sleeping rough anywhere they could.

 David and I did not want to leave our wonderful home and our residents but David was doing the giant's share of the work and we both needed a break to recharge our batteries. We arranged for Liz to take over, only taking our personal belongings with us. We passed over Sunnycroft in good faith, leaving everything behind, lock, stock and barrel. We didn't want to lose Sunnycroft. It was an asset to the Council, to the all the services, and to all the homeless people of Mansfield. It was the shock of Uncle Cyril taking his own life. The impact it had on my life and my health was devastating.

One of my young residents, Stan, with my
sister's son, Paul, and Vulcan, our donkey at Sunnycroft
in 1975

Sunnycroft was a beautiful house and I will always have
memories of how hard David worked to support me.

# CHAPTER 10

# HANBURY COURT

We moved into Hanbury Court on the Oak Tree Lane estate with Andy, Paul, Lynn and David junior. We struggled to furnish it. The house was a four bedroom semi-detached. Our neighbours, Fred and Rose, moved in a few days later. They had four children around the same age as ours. Melanie was the same age as David Junior. We got on well with Fred and Rose, and the children got on well together. Melanie and David Junior became close. They were playing in the garden one day when David got stung by a bee. His face swelled up like a balloon, his eyes were swollen and a jelly-like substance was in his eyes. We took him to hospital thinking he'd had an allergic reaction to the bee sting, only to learn that he had a bad case of hay fever, caused by the mown grass. Since leaving Sunnycroft David Junior was catching everything going.

We hadn't been there long when we got involved with helping in the community. The school had been flooded and needed support to raise funds. Although I was still struggling with my health I started a keep-fit class in the school hall. I could not believe how well it took off. I had a very good turnout and the class grew. I bought Eileen Fowler records and learned every move and every dance step myself before introducing them to all the ladies who joined. We had a large class and it was expanding. I organised a ten mile sponsored walk, with the entire fund going to the school. I led the walk and everyone finished - no one dropped out. We also had outside games when the weather permitted and had some fun playing rounders and football. Mrs Haywood was a wonderful headmistress and got involved with the fundraising.

Doing the keep-fit classes had improved my health: I was back to myself and wanted to return to my role of caring for and working with the homeless. David felt exactly the same. He got involved in charity work through his singing, together with Walter Jones, the landlord of the Sir Winston pub in Annesley Woodhouse, near Kirkby-in Ashfield. Walter's brother, Barry, Chad (a compère), Councillor Frank Haynes and Tim Oats of the Blind Association in Nottingham got together to raise funds for a minibus to help the blind people of Nottinghamshire. They formed a group of singers and entertainers called the Winston Show Group. The group were all volunteers, giving their time and talents for free. Bill was on the drums, Frank was on the organ, and there were many more, including versatile Betty, Barry "Elvis", Mary and Roy - a husband and wife duet, all from Kirkby. Tom Bell of Nottingham Taxis, Pam who was a professional singer and our Rosie from The Midland playing the piano. They travelled round the clubs and pubs of Ashfield, Nottinghamshire and Derbyshire. Dave put on a concert for the Oak Tree Lane School fund, setting up in the school hall. Mrs Haywood couldn't thank everyone enough. We also helped Social Services and Probation by taking in homeless young people temporarily until they could find accommodation. After a year both Paul and Lynn were working.

We had a phone call from Liz, the lady we let take over Sunnycroft. She told us that Sue, one of the residents we had looked after for many years, was in hospital: her lungs had collapsed. David and I went straight to the hospital to see Sue, who was on a machine. When she saw us she cried. She told us that she had missed us and wanted us back at Sunnycroft. We explained to her that we couldn't take it back off Liz, we had passed it over in good faith. Sue said she didn't want to go back to Sunnycroft. I could see by David's face he was deep in thought. He told Sue that if she got herself better then he would come and fetch her, to take her back home with us. At that, Sue said, "Does that mean I can come and live back with you?

David said, "Yes Sue, I promise you - if you get yourself better, that is exactly what I mean." We continued to visit Sue and she made a marvellous recovery. As promised, David brought her home.

Then Steven, who had also lived with us for many years, came up to see us. We didn't have enough room to take him in but we told him he could come up for a meal and visit. So Steven started to come up every week. Social Services rang me to see if we could help another young man by taking him in temporarily until they could find him accommodation. We took him in for a few weeks and they found him lodgings. I took in another resident - a young girl - until accommodation could be found for her. Fortunately one of our neighbours had a spare room and they gave her a home.

My sister-in-law, Barbara, had got re-married to a lovely man, John, who had his own work yard on King Street, off Newgate Lane. He had a little caravan where he could make himself a meal, and his guests and customers tea or coffee. I called John "Mr Magic". He was the best mechanic in Mansfield and he would always come and help David out if we had any problems with our car. It was a bonus that I was close to my brother Frank's children, Susan and Ian, plus her other two children, Lynn and Dean. Another good thing was that David and I were there at a time when Barbara and John were struggling financially and we were able to support them. We made sure they had a good Christmas. We got Christmas presents for my nephews and nieces and made sure they had food on the table, although we were finding things difficult at the same time.

Barbara and I will be friends for life. John unfortunately passed away and I haven't seen my niece, Sue, for many years since she got married and became a nurse.

Another fond memory of my time at Hanbury Court was when I motivated all the neighbours to decorate the streets, and to organise a street party for the wedding of Charles and Diana.

Once, school phoned me to say that David had had an accident and cut his ear very deeply on the corner of a desk. I felt sick when I went down to school and saw the blood. I could do anything for other children but when my own children were hurt it always affected me differently. I took David to the hospital but couldn't watch them stitch his ear as I knew I would pass out. After that I got another call from the school to say David had caught the nevus on his foot that was like a birth mark. They couldn't stop the bleeding. I rang the doctors' surgery for advice and they told me to put ice cubes on his foot to stop the bleeding. After it had bled, a fleshy tree-like growth was developing on his foot and he couldn't stand wearing a shoe. It kept growing and I had to take him up to Forest Hospital for a doctor to cauterize it to stop it growing back. I wondered what else was going to happen to David - it was obvious he was going to be accident prone!

At around the same time I filled in an application for the post of warden at Lochbuie, and David applied for the relief warden's post. We were shortlisted and asked to go for an interview at the Council's Carr Bank offices. On the day of the interview our appointment was for 10am. We arrived at 9.45 and found there were quite a lot of applicants. I was around the sixth to go in. Mr Laurence Fletcher, Mrs Bebbington and Mr Price interviewed me. I knew Mr Fletcher from my days at Sunnycroft. He asked me, "Mary, put your cards on the table. Would you take the post of warden without David?"

I said, "No, David and I are used to working together; I wouldn't want to take it without him." The interview carried on with Mrs Bebbington and Mr Price asking me a lot of questions. They thanked me, shook hands and said they would let me know. David was the next in. I sat in the waiting room - there were still a few more people waiting to be interviewed. Everyone in the waiting room must have heard David making Mr Fletcher, Mrs Bebbington and Mr Price laugh. When we got outside I said, "What did you say to them?" He said he'd just shared a joke with them. I said to David, "Before we go home, let's go up to Uncle Walter's for a cup of tea - Uncle Walter was another one of my dad's brothers. When we arrived back home it was around 1.30pm. To our surprise, a letter had been put through the letterbox. David picked it up and read it. He was smiling and excited. He said, "We had better go straight back to Carr Bank: we've got another appointment at 2pm with Mr Clark." He asked us how we would feel having to take separate holidays. We told him we very rarely had holidays together as our work had been demanding. He asked me how I would sort out the accommodation as we had two flats. I explained that the lower flat could be a living area, bathroom, kitchen and bedroom for David and myself, also using it as a office. The upstairs flat would be used as just bedrooms, kitchen and bathroom. He looked at David and then asked, "How soon can you move in?" I asked him about the notice on our present address. He said, "Don't worry about that, we will sort it out; will you move in on Monday?" He said the Council had no problems with David and me keeping the two foster children with us; it would be okay for them to move into Lochbuie as part of the family. In fact we didn't have to worry about Andy. He had moved on to live with Anne and they were planning to get married, leaving us with only Sue to worry about.

On the same day we got our post with Mansfield Council, we also received the keys to Lochbuie. That was on a Friday. On the Saturday, David went down and decorated the sitting room-cum-office. On the Sunday we moved into our new accommodation ready to start work on the Monday morning. Paul and Lynn had gone to work. David took David Junior up to Oak Tree School as we did not have time to transfer him to Newgate Lane School. David Junior would be five on his next birthday so we decided to let him stay on a while at Oak Tree with his teacher and friends. We were so pleased to be back caring for the homeless people of Mansfield and surrounding areas again.

# CHAPTER 11

# LOCHBUIE

On our first day at Lochbuie, Mrs Moxon came up to introduce herself to us. She was the Mansfield District Housing Officer over all the wardens of sheltered housing. She was amazed that David had decorated the sitting room-cum-office and that we had moved in and got straight, ready to start work. Mrs Moxon had been updated on our ability to run the hostel and on our experience. We had a cup of tea while we discussed our duties. I explained to Mrs Moxon that she could trust us, that we would work with the families who were already in residence; we would introduce ourselves and let them come to us if they needed our support. The hostel needed a lot of work and the grounds needed attention. The gardeners who worked for the Council used the outhouse for their lunch breaks. They worked for the Parks Department at the bottom of Park Avenue. They only mowed the lawns, they were not responsible for weeding and digging the gardens. Our plan was to clean the whole hostel and bring it up to a high standard before tackling the grounds. We decided to set an example to the residents as we believed that setting an example was better than exercising authority. It wasn't long before the residents joined in with us. I was bleaching and cleaning all the bathrooms and toilets, washing all the walls and paintwork down, and scrubbing the communal corridors. David was checking all the maintenance and repairs that needed to be done.

I was pleased to see Mrs Ashley. She was our neighbour when we lived at Sunnycroft and she waved as she saw us moving in. I told her I would be over to see her after work. So I popped over to have a chat and a cup of tea with her. I was on my way back home when I heard some shouting. It was two of the residents falling out over their children. I asked them to come to the office for a cup of tea. I thought it would be better than leaving it to get out of control. I explained to them that while they were falling out, their children would be making friends again. By the time they went back to the flats they were okay.

We had another resident who was buying and selling cars - that was not our problem. However, he was repairing them on the car park in front of Lochbuie. I had to explain that the Council would give him notice to vacate his flat as repairing cars in the grounds was not allowed. If we let him get away with it, it would give the wrong message to other residents. He said he had always done it before we came. David came out of the office. He told the resident the truth: the same rules applied to us and he should read the terms and conditions on his temporary accommodation agreement. He came to the office and apologised for the mess he had made on the car park.

In our first month we faced some really rough families. We just stood firm. We didn't bother the Council; we handled the problems in a very fair way. We had a meeting with the residents to let them know that we respected their views and would do anything in our power to make their stay at the hostel a pleasant experience, and that because they were homeless we were only there to help and support them. We told them to make sure they always saved their receipts after paying their rent, as that covered us and them. Dealing with families was very different from dealing with the single homeless; they had to take responsibility for dealing with their own problems, as adults, and take responsibility for their children. If they needed our support, we were there for them. The children always used to wave to David and myself and we loved the children - that was a bonus as some very lovely children came into the hostel. We would ask family and friends if they would donate any toys or clothing. We used to keep sweets and biscuits in the office to treat the children as most of our residents struggled on a low income. We wanted to lift their morale and do everything to make their stay at the hostel as pleasant as we possibly could.

We had a lot of single parent families. Mothers would turn up at the hostel at all times of day and night. We would often listen to their stories, some heartbreaking. We made them feel welcome and always had the kettle on. We were dedicated to our work and we cared. We were there to help them get back onto their feet. I remember saying to so many, "You are at rock bottom now and there is only one way to go, and that is back up."

Mrs Bebbington used to call in to see how we were doing. She was very pleased to see that the residents and their families were already trusting David and myself. A few weeks later Mr Hind came round with members of the Labour Party - they were doing their annual check. I wasn't surprised to see some familiar faces: Mr Fletcher, Cllor K Williams, Cllor J Hawkins, Cllor M Gallagher, etc. They spoke to both David and myself and thanked us for all our hard work. Families were coming and going and getting re-housed as soon as a vacancy was available. David and I got an invitation to a meeting at the Manor House at Woodhouse. All the top people of the Council were there. We already knew Mr Hind, Mr Fletcher, Mr Price, Mrs Bebbington, Mrs Betts, etc. At this time I was introduced to Mr D Littler and Mr I Saville who both became very supportive of David, me and our residents. We were told that the Council offices were going to be relocated on to Chesterfield Road, so that the Council services would all be in one building. They hadn't got a date but it was in the pipeline.

David was still doing his charity work with the Winston Show Group and I was still doing my keep fit up at Oak Tree School. David Junior was at Newgate Lane School and the Head Mistress, Mrs Ploughwright, and David's teacher asked me to consider starting up a keep fit class at their school. I did start the keep fit group and it went well. David put on a charity night for the school. We entered the "Mr and Mrs" contest - it was really funny. We didn't do badly - we agreed on five out of the six questions that Mrs Ploughwright had set.

I was working 24/7 again and I was being paid a salary based on a 38 ½ hour week. I never claimed for the overtime or unsocial hours when I was called out during the night. If a family used to come in late and they had nothing for the children, David and I would give them teabags, milk, sugar, bread, butter and cereals for the children's breakfast. I would help the families fill in all their forms for benefits, give them letters to get help with clothing grants, and ring local schools to take their children on a temporary basis till the family got re-housed. I worked with Roundwood Surgery to get them medical help in emergencies - they couldn't register with a doctor until they got a permanent address. I was co-ordinating with all the public services and my job title was changed from Warden to Co-ordinator. I had earned this title and was made a member of staff.

At the time the Civic Centre was being built on Chesterfield Road, Mrs E Betts, Mrs K Fullwood and Mr I Saville were very supportive colleagues. Liz, who had taken over Sunnycroft, had suddenly passed away. The council re-housed all the residents. We were worried that we would lose Sunnycroft. Thankfully the Council made Sunnycroft into flats, giving us more units for the homeless. Again the plight of the homeless was escalating. We still had the three hostels and all the hostels and warden-controlled housing were connected up to the central control system. I trained the new wardens and taught them how to do the books, rents and benefits. I had set up my own filing system on A-Z records in 1985.

Also in 1985 I did a charity walk for St Peter's Church to help with the work on the church roof: it was in desperate need of restoration. I walked from a little village in South Wales, Deri, near Cardiff, back to Mansfield, over 200 miles by road. I followed the A-roads, walking over the hills of the valley roads on to Abergavenny, Tredegar, Kidderminster, Stroud, Dudley, Derby, Lichfield, Chesterfield, Alfreton, Sutton in Ashfield and Mansfield. The following year my friends, Barbara and Vi, walked the Pennine way with me for the hospice charity. We stayed in the YHA hostels. We started at Edale, then to Crowden, Mankinholes, Haworth, Earby, Malham, Hawes, Keld, Baldersdale, Dufton, Alston, Once Brewed, Bellingham and Byrness, finishing at Kirk Yetholm. Edgar Peel booked all the hostels right through for us. He got the distance wrong on our second lap and we had to get help from Peter, Barbara's husband, arriving late at Mankinholes. Then it went wrong again and Vi's husband came to our aid. After that things went well, until I bought a new pair of hiking boots in Hawes: they crippled me but I carried on regardless.

One day as we came off track we found a young ram trapped. It had fallen into a hole and couldn't get out. Barbara tried to lift it out but it was too heavy. I said to Barbara, "Try to coax it nearer to the edge." I stood with my legs braced firmly either side of the hole, grabbed its horns, pulled it up as hard as I could and managed to get it free. Its mother had been waiting nearby and the little ram ran off towards her. We went back up the grassy hill and got back on track. We met some other hikers and became friends so we all walked on together.

There was one hiker they called "the Flying Scotsman". He passed us on the way up. I tried to bed in my boots again but to no avail - they really hurt my feet. I was so angry I threw them away. Barbara retrieved them for me. When we reached Once Brewed we got a bunk bed and I took the top bunk. Climbing up the ladder I injured my foot but there was no way I was going to give up at this stage. I walked as far as I could the next day but the pain was agony. I asked Barbara and Vi if they would continue on to Bellingham and I would meet them there. I had to catch the bus, which was only a short journey. When they arrived I had sorted out the meal and drinks.

The next leg was through Burness Forest to Jedburgh. When we got through the forest we stopped to check our route. I helped Vi back on with her rucksack; she helped me with mine. Poor Barbara, we walked off without thinking. Vi and I sat down for a cigarette on the roadside and Barbara came striding past us, giving us a glare and said, "And I love you too." When we got to the hostel Barbara had everything ready for us (bless), then we heard a voice saying, "Are you ladies coming for a drink?" It was the Flying Scotsman. He was on his way back down the Pennine Way. We were too tired, all we wanted to do was to get a good night's sleep.

We had to walk to Usway Ford the next day, the halfway point of our last lap - our last night on the Pennine Way. We were in the wilderness looking for a farmhouse and wondering if we were going to have to sleep rough. There was a winding road and we couldn't see the end. I left Barbara and Vi and went down a banking to look around. Bingo! I spotted the farmhouse. It was really rough and dirty because the farmer was ill with cancer. We had to make our own tea. We didn't feel like eating anything and went to our room. We just got up the next morning and went on our way, our last day of the walk. We met up with a party of soldiers who were on their way down the Pennines. They made us some bacon sandwiches and cups of tea. We really did appreciate their kindness. We walked for another four hours and reached Kirk Yetholm and got a lift to the famous pub on the other side of the village. There was a large oak tree in full bloom. We were having a drink and something to eat when I spotted David, my husband, lying in the sun under the tree waiting to take us home. I had lost two stone in weight and was as fit as a fiddle. All three of us looked like we had spent a week abroad in a hot country, we were that suntanned. Apparently a search party had been out looking for us one night when we were late arriving at our hostel - we were the talk of the Pennine Way. We had laughed and cried, and Vi had become known as the "bog queen". She sank in the bogs and had to leave her shoes underneath all the mud.

Back at work after the walk I had some new residents; they were a big family. I gave them Flat 7, facing the office. On occasions I could smell something on the landing outside their flat that I had smelt before when some girls had brought in some drugs. Betty's two boys used to go into their flat. Betty was one of the residents I had known for many years. We met when we were teenagers at a party for the Queen's coronation in 1953. I didn't see her again until she turned up at Lochbuie, homeless, with her triplets, Sue, John and David. I told Betty of my concerns about drugs on the property. She told me that the resident in Flat 7 had given her a packet to save for him. Now I was more concerned for Betty and her boys. She gave me the packet when I asked and I knew straight away that it was cannabis. It was in a blue wrapper. I told Betty that if the police raided the flats and found this she could lose her children and get a prison sentence. She gave me the packet and told me to take it.

I rang the Council and spoke to Ian Saville. I explained that I had been suspicious that drugs were being brought on to the property. Ian asked me to go down to the Council with the package. When I got to the Civic Centre he said, "Are you sure its drugs, Mary?" I said I thought so. Ian rang the police. When they turned up Ian gave them the packet to check. The police confirmed it was a block of cannabis. I had to go to the police station to give a statement. Betty was also asked to give a statement. They asked Betty if she had ever taken drugs. Betty was so frightened she put her cigarettes on the desk and told the officer she only smoked Berkley. They let Betty go and then arrested the resident from Flat 7. I had to face him: I told him straight not to blame Betty, that I was the one that reported the drugs to the police and that I had a duty to protect my residents. I went back home and told David what had happened as he had been admitting a new resident. I was expecting trouble from the resident's son in Flat 7, but the resident came to my office and told me he was sorry for bringing the drugs into the hostel. He said he appreciated that I was straight with him about me reporting the matter. We let it go and put it behind us. This family went into Derbyshire, picked up a lamb and brought it back to their flat as a pet. When the Council told them to get it out of their flat, they refused. They were re-housed to Woodhouse and took the lamb with them.

David and I had to go on courses. We went to the Civic Theatre on Leeming Street for First Aid training. To my surprise the training officer was Mr Weaver, a friend of my dad's from the days I used to go with him up to Crown Farm Pit. Mr Weaver was the "pit bobby", as we called him, and a police officer serving Forest Town. We had some fun on First Aid and we all passed and got our certificates. I was also going up to the Council offices on Chesterfield Road, which had been specially built since the meeting we went to at the manor house. At the Civic I met a lot of Council staff and worked with them. I got on well with most of them and saw them as friends as well as colleagues. Sheila Clapham used to help me with her computer: she would log me on and teach me. Sheila was always the same. I still keep in touch with her and several others: Emily Betts, Marian Curr, Sue, Joyce Bostock, Helen Anderson, Kath Fullwood and Maureen Bailey. Maureen went to the same school as I did, Riversdale. It was a pleasure to work with all of them.

At the hostel David and I put on a garden party for residents, neighbours, friends and family to raise funds for a swing to put up in the grounds for the residents' children. David brought his friends from the Winston Show Group. They staged a show under the patio that led off Flat 3 at the back of the grounds. Mrs Betts sold programmes at the entrance gate, Mrs Moxon was selling ice creams, I was selling teas, coffees and hot dogs from the office kitchen, and Lynn, my daughter, was selling baked potatoes. The residents were selling hot peas with mint sauce from Flat 1 which was on the front grounds of the building. There was seating on the back lawn which the Council had loaned to us from one of the centres. Mr Hind and other officials came from the Civic Centre, as did Frank Haynes - MP for Ashfield. Brunt's School had a garden party on the same day so some of their visitors were drifting on to ours. "Mr Splash", who raised a lot of money for charities, came to visit us; all the children were delighted. Mrs J Robinson and her children came over - they were our neighbours on The Park across the road from Lochbuie. Mr and Mrs P O'Gorman were also our neighbours. When the Show Group started, everyone was getting involved, joining in with the singing, dancing, etc. It was a great day and a great evening which everyone enjoyed. The Council sent down some of the park workers to concrete the swing into the ground to make it safe.

My daughter, Lynn, was now married with three children, Nicole (4), Donna (3), and Daniel (2). Paul, my son, was in the armed forces in Germany, and Andrew was married to Anne. They have two lovely sons, Martin and Lee. Had my friend, Janet, lived, I know she would have been so proud. David Junior was growing into a very active 10-year-old. He was still at Newgate Lane School and had made friends with the neighbours' children. We had a good community and were there for each other.

That year we got a family in who ran riot through the hostel. They wouldn't stick to the Council's rules and refused to pay their rent. David told me to just record everything. Their son, who was a lot older, kicked young David and he had to be admitted to hospital for an operation. One evening when their daughter was very poorly they came to our door for help. I went over and they let me into their flat. I could see that the little girl had got a fever: she was burning up and covered in sweat, her little face was flushed. I wasn't sure what was wrong but I knew we needed to get her to hospital. I told them to wrap her in a blanket and bring her to the front door of the hostel. I ran back to get David and told him to pull up as close as he could to the front door of Lochbuie. We told her mum and dad to get into the back seats of the car with her and we drove them straight up to Kings Mill Hospital. I went into the Accident and Emergency Department and explained to the staff on duty that I was very worried about the little girl who, by now, was having difficulty breathing. The child was rushed through and had to be put on oxygen. Both David and I waited with the parents. We got them a cup of tea then sat with them till we got the results. The doctors told them they were lucky; their little girl had got pneumonia and was very poorly. The mum stayed over at the hospital and we gave the dad a lift back with us. That family changed overnight. They came to thank us and told us the little girl had to stay in hospital until her temperature came down - it was still high.

I was put in the same position by a young mum whose baby was only just over nine months old. She was a single mum in Flat 4 and came to me very worried. When I checked the baby I knew I needed to get help. I rang Dr Golshetti and he came straight down to the hostel. He confirmed that the baby could have pneumonia. He asked David to take the mum and baby up to the hospital in our car as it would be quicker than waiting for an ambulance. A few days later when the baby came home I couldn't believe what I was seeing: this mum was walking outside with the baby who had nothing on its little feet. I said to her, "Do you want your baby back in hospital? Go and put something on her feet."

It was coming up to winter and we were already thinking about Christmas. We used to get little presents for the children who were in the hostel over the Christmas period. Ian Saville used to come up to the hostel with mince pies and a couple of bottles of wine for the residents, and selection boxes for the children. David always dressed up as Santa Claus.

Geoff Lane, who was the chief executive of the Council, used to come up to the hostel and say to me, "Mary, where's your old man?"

I'd say, "He's around somewhere."

"I'll find him," Geoff would say, and go in search of David. He came up to talk to us about what was needed to complete the homeless units. We told him it would be nice if we could get somewhere for single people and a single parent with one child. He promised us he would sort it out. True to his word, Geoff set up a purpose-built hostel, Stonecross Court, built on the corner of Crow Hill Drive and Woodhouse Road. Now we had three hostels and a refuge for women and children fleeing violence. Seven flats at Sunnycroft, nine flats at Lochbuie, four flats at Oakdene and 12 units at Stonecross. Mansfield had the best homeless provision in the country.

In 1970 I had made those two promises to Janet which I had kept and still worked towards achieving. There is no way I could have done this on my own without the help of so many professional people. It was amazing to have all the services working together for the same cause, people who went above and beyond their call of duty for some of the most vulnerable people who lived in Mansfield and surrounding areas. All these people and their families can be proud.

David and I could settle down now and continue working within the field of caring. Canon Warburton of St Peter and St Paul's Church helped homeless people who were passing through Mansfield. He used to send them to me with a supporting letter when he needed help and I always managed to get them accommodation somehow, so that I wouldn't let him down. In the winter months he would open the church hall and everyone would rally round and support him. Another local lady, who was always helping the homeless people of Mansfield, was Nita and her husband Ron. They owned Steptoe's Parlour on Westfield Lane. When my residents came to be re-housed they only got a certain amount of money from Social Security to cover basic needs, e.g. beds, bedding, pots and pans, cutlery, cooker and fridge. Mr Manning from Social Security used to pay Nita and Ron for furniture. Nita was very soft-hearted and would give them the bedding free or some extra help by giving them a washer. Nita still helps people that are needy. Her husband, Ron, passed away eight years ago. Nita is still working in her shop at the bottom of Somersall Street, and still helping the people of Mansfield out. She once found two young homeless girls on the fields off Westhill Lane and brought them up to me at Lochbuie. They were too young to be wandering the streets. I rang the Social Services and a social worker came up to talk to them. They asked me to keep the girls with me in the office until they sorted things out. Next thing the police turned up. They spoke to the girls and found out that they had run away from home. The police thanked me for contacting the Social Services. The girls were taken back home safely to their parents. If Nita hadn't brought them to me who knows where they would have ended up: children don't see danger.

During this year David let me go on holiday to the Miners' Holiday Camp in Skegness. I took David Junior, Nicole and Donna. We all had a great holiday and met Maureen, Mick, their son Mark and daughter Maz, entertainers known as "The All Family Affair". Maureen played the keyboard and Mick the drums. Mark also played the keyboard and Maz was a singer like her mum. We have stayed friends all these years, they are like family. Mark and Maz are both married now and Maureen and Mick live in Great Yarmouth. They have done lots of charity work over the years and are very genuine friends. They were also well known as "Dolly Daydream and Micko the Clown" and worked as children's entertainers at Summerland's in Skegness for many years.

When I got back home I was knocked up in the early hours of the morning by a resident from Flat 9. He said, "My wife's in labour, can you come?"

I shouted up to David, "We've got an emergency!" I ran all the way to their flat and saw that the baby was on the bed, still in the water sac. I told the father to ring my friend Audrey. I wrote her number down and then told him to ring for an ambulance. I burst the sac that the baby was in and lifted the baby out. I gently rubbed its back to get it breathing. It started to cry so I knew it was alive. I had never seen a baby so small. I wrapped it in a towel to keep it warm. Then I saw another baby was coming - I could see its feet so I knew it was breach. I told the mum not to push as I knew that the cord could be round its neck. I delivered the second baby just as Audrey arrived. She contacted the hospital to send incubators for the babies. I went back over to the office and David had come on duty in case I needed any help. I had left the mum and babies in the care of the professionals. I told David to make me a cup of tea. It was 7.30am. The ambulance left Lochbuie with the lights flashing. Audrey came to the office and we had a cup of tea together. Later that day the press turned up; they had spoken to the residents who had told them I was the hero of the day. I told them the mum was the hero of the day. I never thought I would ever deliver a baby, let alone twins. I got cards from staff and from another midwife, Judy Dutton, saying, "Well done, Mary, come and join us, we are short of midwives!" I still have the cards and paper cutting today.

I had to get the spare key to Flat 5 as I was worried about another resident - a young mum with a new baby. She had asked a neighbour to watch her baby as she was feeling sick. I hadn't seen her around. I was told to wait for the police to come but didn't know how long it would take. I couldn't wait, so I got another resident to go into the flat with me. The young mum was lying on the bed; she had been very sick and she was cold and clammy. I thought it might be something serious so I went to call her GP, who was Dr Christener. I didn't know what was wrong but she had been abroad with her mum on holiday, and told me she had been suffering with headaches since she got back. There were some tablets in her flat but not many - no empty pill boxes or bottles lying around, which ruled out her trying to take an overdose. Dr Christener sent for an ambulance. With the information I was able to give him he told me he thought it might be meningitis. She was a very lucky girl, as it was indeed meningitis. Going to bed and locking her flat door without telling anyone could have cost her her life.

After this David had to retire because of his age - he was 72. This meant the Council would have to employ another warden to work with me. Pauline, one of my ex-residents, got the post and she lived just down the road on Baggaley Crescent. She was my relief worker. Pauline knew the job so all I had to train her in was the filing system, the rent books, receipts and paperwork. Pauline was also made the relief warden for Oakdene. She covered both hostels and we made a rota so everyone knew days off and holidays. This was good for me and David as it meant we could have nights out together and take our holiday together. Pauline was always fair: she would clean the flats and bathrooms and do the corridors. We became a team with Margaret from Oakdene and little Janice from Stonecross. There was a new warden at Sunnycroft named Caroline. We had been working with a new manager, Kay Wainman, Mrs Betts having retired. Kay was a good manager. Unfortunately she moved on but gave me a lovely card thanking me for all my hard work.

David and I had been looking to foster a young 15-year-old called Paul who was at The Ridge children's home - a large house on Ridgeway at the back of Lochbuie. Paul was a young boy with learning disabilities who we had taken to. At Christmas we had put on a Christmas party for the children at The Ridge. In 1990 David and I applied to the Adult Placement Scheme run by Notts County

Council. Trevor Lewis, a social worker, came to do a home study on our suitability to offer a home to Paul. We were duly approved. Paul used to come for the weekends at first, so that he could get to know us and to see if he could settle down into our family. Both David Junior and Paul were eager for this to happen and Paul moved in permanently with us. He had his own social worker, Janet Wiggins. She had taken him to her own home for Christmas and Paul told us how much he had enjoyed himself with Janet's family. Paul and David Junior got on very well together. Paul attended Worksop College. Transport was arranged to pick him up and drop him off back at home after college, so we knew he was in safe hands. David put everything into teaching Paul, and Paul became very close to all the family. He asked if he could call us Mum and Dad: we told him we felt proud that he had accepted us to be his parents. He still calls me Mum today. Since meeting Trevor and going on training courses I have had the pleasure of meeting Pam, his lovely wife. We have become friends and have spent social times together. Trevor is helping me with my book and has helped me on many occasions.

My son in Germany had married Melanie, a German girl. I went over for their wedding in Duisburg. A few months later they gave us the good news that we were to become grandparents again. He had married into a lovely family who made me very welcome and treated Paul like their own son.

We were told that Paul (the other Paul, now placed with us) would possibly never live independently, but Paul has progressed since becoming a member of our family and is now living independently in his own flat and comes home on a regular basis. I think David Junior had a lot of influence in helping Paul to become independent. We bought Paul a mountain bike and David Junior a second-hand three-wheeled petrol quad bike. It never let him down: one push, the engine started and it was away. He used to drive it round giving his friends a "backy".

One of the residents was always very nasty towards other residents and the children, always shouting out of his flat window for the children to clear off. The back lawns were the children's play area; it was safe for them and parents could keep an eye on their children.

David Junior, Paul, and their friends on the park had their own little football team. David Junior used to arrange a match with Gavin, one of the workers at The Ridge. One week they would play on The Ridge grounds, another week they would play at Lochbuie. George, who was the caretaker at Brunt's School, gave the boys a set of football nets. His son, Matthew, was in David Junior's team and they used the nets when they played their matches. It was good for the residents' children as they were allowed to join in. Gavin always supervised the two teams so things never got out of control.

The resident who was always complaining and shouting at the children was out of order. We tried to talk to him but he didn't want to be reasonable or try to co-operate in any way. This resident had had problems with the Council and had been abusive to some of the Council staff. I believe he was doing it to try and get re-housed faster, but it didn't wash with the Council and David and I were used to people like him. We didn't let him get away with trying to bully us or the other residents. One Sunday morning we were doing breakfast for the boys before coming on duty, when fire engines and police cars came through the entrance of Lochbuie. We had not received any calls from the Council to let us know anything was wrong. I went down to find out what the problem was. I spoke to a police officer. He told me the bomb squad had been called by the resident in Flat 6 (the resident that was always complaining). There was nothing I could do, only wait.

The bomb squad officer was smiling; he said whoever made this little device was clever. He showed me something that resembled batteries and a clock face. Someone had fastened it to the window ledge of Flat 6. The next thing I knew the resident had packed all his belongings and left! I told David and the boys when I went back upstairs. We had no idea who could have done this.

Our new manager was Becky. I had to send for her to come and see me because David had taken ill and I was very worried about him. Then Audrey called in early one morning. I had suffered with haemorrhoids for many years, without seeking help. David told Audrey he was worried about me as I had been in the bathroom a long time. Audrey knocked on the bathroom door and asked me if anything was wrong. I didn't want to open the door as my haemorrhoids had burst. I was trying to clean up all the blood: it had sprayed everywhere. Audrey asked me to let her in. I opened the bathroom door and when she saw the blood she said, "Mary that is your life blood. I am going to the surgery, I have to tell one of the doctors."

I padded myself up and went down to start work. I got a phone call from Doctor Overy who said, "Don't you stay at work, I want you to come to the surgery as soon as you can." I went straight down to the surgery and was told that I would have to have an operation. I explained to him I didn't want to leave David as he had been diagnosed with emphysema. He suggested I had some injections that would shrink the haemorrhoids. He did the injections the same day. They only lasted three months, then I had to go up to the hospital to see Mr Jackaman. He wanted me in as soon as possible. David was still very poorly. Lynn said she would keep dropping in to check on her dad. I decided to go ahead with the operation. Mr Jackaman told me they had a new method. Instead of cutting out the haemorrhoids he was now doing the operations using a laser treatment. My sister, Jacky, was there for me along with my daughter Lynn. Canon Warburton sent up Sonia from the church to visit me. After the operation I only stayed in hospital for two days, I was more worried about David. He was struggling to breathe. He was also worrying about me.

Soon after I got out of hospital I had to send for the doctor for David and the doctor admitted him to hospital. David wasn't eating. When I got to the hospital to visit him I found him hanging out of the bed with his feet touching the floor. I told Lynn and Carl, my son-in-law, to bring David back home for me. Carl carried David up the stairs of our flat. He was only back at home for two weeks. I had put up the Christmas tree and decorations; David loved Christmas. A gas bottle with a breathing mask was delivered and brought in by the chemist as David was struggling for breath. Betty, with the triplets who had been both a friend and resident, came up to help me the night before David passed away. Betty watched David for me. I slept at the side of David with my arms round him, so that he knew I was there. The next night David got worse. I sent for the doctor. It was Dr Steiner who came and I went downstairs to talk to him. I told him I knew that I was going to lose David. Dr

Steiner said to call him if I needed him in the night. Lynn went to fetch Jane, David's daughter. David asked me to give him a kiss. I gave him a kiss and as I lifted my head back up he stroked my face. I saw one tear roll down his face. He told me he loved me. They were his last words. I felt sick and went to the bathroom. When I returned David took his last breaths. The only consolation was that David had seen a photo of his new granddaughter, Jacqueline, Paul and Melanie's daughter. That was the 12th of December 1991.

I wrote my dedication to him which I will share with you.

## OH MY SWEET BELOVED DAVID

I worship and loved you too much
I will always remember your last kiss
Your last gentle touch
We had many happy memories together
I always thought you would be with me forever
No one will ever take your place - you were my life
You were my husband I was your wife
We two were always one
You gave to me a precious son
Whenever I needed you, you were always there
My troubles, my pains you would always share
Every morning my cup of tea in bed
Your words of wisdom always said
What more could I have really wanted
You carried me and I took you for granted
Your patience and understanding never wearing
You were so faithful so loving so caring
My love for you will never die
Inside my heart I will always cry
We will not be parted by your death
I will always love you forever until my last breath

All our family and friends attended David's funeral. Representing the Council were Geoff Lane, Ian Saville, Becky Rance, Margaret Cotton and Pauline Meehan. David's Winston Show Group friends attended: Barry Jones, Mr and Mrs Roy Wright and others. Canon Warburton conducted the service at the church and by the graveside.

It took me a long time to get over losing him but I started back at work. Poor Paul, he thought he would have to leave because I had lost David. I had to explain to him that he wasn't going anywhere - he was staying with us. David Junior and Paul just grew closer, they were like real brothers. David always tried to protect Paul, although he was still only 15 himself. I took Paul to Germany with us, to Paul and Melanie's. He really enjoyed himself, he loved the German food. Then we took him to Kassiopi in Greece with Lynn, Carl, David and my three grandchildren.

Work was getting more and more demanding. Caroline was the warden at Stonecross and Shirley came as a relief worker. We got put on to a rota system: I was covering Sunnycroft and Oakdene on Margaret's days off and holidays. Pauline was having a bad time as her husband, Joe, was suffering with his legs. Shirley didn't get on with Caroline and she felt that she was being put on. Me, I just carried on regardless. I managed to get the

Council to make the workmen's room into a washroom with a washer and dryer to help out the residents. It made it better for us as well. The laundry from the flats was always mounting up after families had vacated their accommodation, though we did have spare bedding for emergencies.

Young David was like me, he was always climbing and he had always been very active. I was off duty and I overheard Pauline saying to young David, "Your mum is going to kill you." Obviously I went down to see what he had done. I asked Pauline but she said, "Ask the workmen." They were standing in the car park. I knew them, they were always coming up to do repairs. They leaned back on to their van, looked up at the roof and said, "We are admiring your bird, Mary." I don't know how long that bird had been up on the roof, standing up on top of the TV aerial. What I did know was that David Junior had brought this stuffed stork from school a few weeks earlier and I had told him it was not coming into my flat. I had told him to put it in the large communal dustbin. It wasn't just the bird being up there, it was the fact that he had tied it on to the aerial with one of my bras!

I continued to work. Caroline left and Carol and her husband and two sons moved into Sunnycroft. They had previously been residents at Lochbuie before I lost David.

Carol was a very large lady who found it difficult to walk. She didn't do any cleaning - her husband and sons did the work for her. At the same time, Shirley was working as a part-time relief worker. She was a lovely, caring lady with a heart of gold. She accidentally left her handbag at Carol's flat and money went missing from her purse. Shirley was very upset as she wasn't well off and couldn't afford to lose the money but she was too timid to say anything and let the matter go, counting her losses.

On another occasion, Carol came over to collect the residents' mail from Lochbuie office - all the mail for both hostels was delivered to Lochbuie. About an hour later her son came to my office. He had a box of CDs and said, "Look what my mum has bought, Mary." I was shocked. She had given her son CDs that had been purchased in a resident's name. This was so wrong I had to report the incident. When the matter was dealt with, Carol gave in her resignation and left.

A new warden was sent up to work with me at Lochbuie, training for the position of warden at Oakdene. She told me she was David's daughter's best mate. I got to trust her and thought I knew her. I did everything to help her and we became good friends. I shared a lot of my personal life with her but, actually, she was picking my brains and I was feeding her knowledge. During this time Pauline lost her husband, Joe. All our staff went to the funeral. After the funeral, Pauline was in a car accident with her daughter, Julie. Pauline damaged her spleen and had to have it removed, leaving her with no immune system - no protection against viruses and infections.

This new warden started to join in my social life with friends and family, joining staff on our nights out at The Bull, at the bottom of Woodhouse Road. As with all my other colleagues, I was 100% loyal to this woman. I gave her support and encouragement when she went to take her exams at college and even supported her to get promotion at the Civic Centre. I truly believed she was my friend but the truth proved to be very different.

Now the member of staff from the office over the hostels told me I was moving to Oakdene as it would be "a lot less work for me". I didn't make that decision, it was made for me. Oakdene was to become another chapter in my life but Lochbuie will always be remembered as young David and Paul's home where they spent much of their childhood growing up with me and their dad. No one can take those memories away. I have my own treasured memories and know that wherever I go my husband, David, will always be with me.

Lochbuie had been our home for 14 years. It was a large, Georgian-built, property that had once been a coach house owned by Councillor Robert Barringer. His father was a partner in Barringer, Wallis, Manners & Co who owned the Metal Box Company. This was originally founded in 1860 and taken over by Barringer & Brown in 1887. The house had originally been purchased to house workers coming to work at the factory from Scotland - hence its Scottish name. There was no proper drainage system at Lochbuie or Sunnycroft; the drainage was a cesspool that ran down the right hand side of both properties. As far as I know it is still there!

Lochbuie

My beloved David

This is Barbara, the probation officer mentioned in Chapter 8 - godmother to my oldest granddaughter in 1995. We have been friends for over 45 years. With Canon Warburton after I did the charity walk to raise funds for repair of the church roof.

# CHAPTER 12

# OAKDENE

I moved into Oakdene and began to work with Janice, the warden at Stonecross Court Hostel. Pauline had also moved up to the Civic Centre to work and she came down to relieve occasionally. The whole system had changed and I didn't know what was happening, none of us did. The staff member over the hostels continued to be in my social life. Arthur and Sue Bagley moved into Lochbuie, into the accommodation that was once our family home. Only Arthur was employed by the council - he was given the position of Co-ordinator. My daughter, Lynn, was already the Co-ordinator of Sunnycroft so Lynn was training Arthur. They got on well and worked well together. We all called Arthur "Arch", so that's what I'll call him here. Even though Sue did not work for the Council she helped Arch with the work and befriended the residents. If they had a lot of work on after someone had left a flat dirty, Arch and Sue worked as a team, just as David and I used to. The member of staff was putting more and more pressure on to the co-ordinators, fetching us off our jobs to help up at the Civic Centre.

When we asked questions or wanted answers the staff member would say, "It's on a 'need to know' basis and you don't need to know."

My hostel was full all the time - as one resident left another one came. I loved the fact that I was there for the residents and their children 24/7, as I lived on site in the top flat. My residents knew that if they needed me anytime, day or night, I would make myself available. Oakdene had three family flats and one smaller flat that was for a mother and child. My hostel was a safe house for women and children fleeing violence. If they were feeling down and wanted to share their worries and problems, it was always in confidence.

There were some very sad cases. I always had the kettle on and some nights, after I had finished duty, I would be on my own time voluntarily. I was cleaning the flats and cleaning the grounds. If a flat needed decorating or freshening up I would do it, very often out of my own pocket. If there was an emergency, central control would ring me up: they knew the hours and times I was called out. I also took in Steven through the Adult Placement Scheme, another young man who was desperate for a home. Like Paul, he came to me from The Ridge children's home in The Park. He was at West Notts College. Steven had behaviour problems and a mild learning disability. I had to teach him hygiene and tidiness. It was my job to prepare to him to move on to independence. He loved it when we had family parties and he loved Christmas.

On the morning of Christmas Day my friends Maureen and Micko came. They were professional entertainers and children's entertainers .They dressed up as Santa and his little helper for the children that were in the hostel. Canon Warburton and the congregation of St Peter and Paul's Church collected toys, sweets and clothes for the children of Oakdene. I was so grateful for their help and kindness. On Christmas Day, when all my family came for the Christmas celebrations, I put on a large buffet and invited the residents to join in with us. Micko dressed as a clown and did many magic tricks. The following year the council provided a Santa and donated selection boxes to the children in all the four hostels. It reminded me of the days Ian Saville used to come up to Lochbuie. Steven stayed on with me until he reached 18. He left college with qualifications that he deserved. His tutor, Gary Dodds, put it down to him having found a settled home where he was happy. Steven had already made up his mind that he wanted to go to live back at home with his parents in Durham. He kept in touch with me up until 2002. Some of my old residents still keep in touch with me: Angela and her daughter, Kirsty, Angela's mum and dad, Jacky and her son, Chad, Michelle and many others. When I am in Mansfield shopping I often meet ex-residents and stop for a chat to see how they are getting on.

I had a mother who was deaf and dumb. Two of her children had the same disability but the other, Rosie, was healthy with no problems. The mum could read and write so it was easy for me to communicate with her; she could also lip read in spite of her disabilities. She was a good mum to her children and her flat was always clean. I got the Council to fit a light in the corner of the room, so that if the fire alarm went off the light would flash in her room to warn her she needed to go out of the safety door. When she moved on I helped her with all her forms and benefits.

I had a young mum in Flat 1 who was on drugs. My other residents were frightened of her but she didn't realise what she was doing to them. She had upset one of the other residents and was swearing and slamming the doors, making the whole building shake. I did try to help and support her, but I also explained to her that she could lose her accommodation. She came into my office and threatened to kill me. I told her that if she was going to kill me, she could try now, as there was no time like the present, but if she was going to kill me I wouldn't just stand there and let her. She left my office calling me all the names she could. She then went down to her flat and started on one of the other residents. She was so angry I went down to stop her from harming someone.

The council had to take her to court to evict her from the flats for the safety of other residents and I had to go into court to testify against her. The Council's legal officer, Christine Oliver, went to court with me. When I got to court I saw Mr Aspley - I hadn't seen him for quite a long time. It was nice to know that he still remembered me from my years at Beech Avenue. The magistrate asked me if I would be prepared to take a chance of keeping the young mum (who had threatened to kill me and threatened my other residents) for another night at the hostel. I felt he had thrown the ball into my court. So I threw the ball straight back. I remember saying to the magistrate, "With respect to the court, sir, can you take the chance?" He decided not to and we won our case. I know Mrs Oliver wrote down my words: she was pleased with my response. That same evening the resident came back to collect some belongings she had left in her flat. Her dad was with her and she apologised for her behaviour. Her dad was a lovely man. He told me he would take her home and try to help her to get off drugs. I have met her since and she's won her battle against drugs. When people are on drugs it messes up their whole lives. It's one of the biggest problems facing the world today.

I have to tell you this next story. A lady was sent to me who was a thalidomide victim of the 1960s. She came in a wheelchair. She had no legs and only two small stumps for arms. I got her settled in and had to devise a rope-pull to fit on the door so that she could get out of the building in case of fire. The only way she had of opening the door was by pulling on the rope with her mouth. I felt that the hostel was not an ideal situation for her, she should have been sent to somewhere with care facilities, perhaps a care home. I did help her on many occasions and nurses came in every day to assist her in washing and changing. She went into hospital and caught MRSA. I was moved out of my flat and sent up to Sunnycroft to stay with my daughter. I was told they moved me out for my own protection until this lady was re-housed.

I got on well with my neighbours. Nora was in the bungalow on my right. She was an elderly lady who has now passed away. There was also Richard and Linda Blake (I was very sorry to hear Richard had passed away). Facing me were Frank and Kath Wright. They lived next door to Stonecross Court Hostel. I would go out every week and sweep the fronts. It wasn't any trouble to sweep my neighbours' fronts at the same time. I was working with Janice and her relief, Linda, who came in two days a week, part-time like Pauline. We worked together as a team.

I had promised Caroline before she left Sunnycroft that I would go to Derbyshire to help out at a summer camp for the Derby Children's Friendship Group - a charity which runs camping holidays for needy children. I applied as a volunteer helper and got the job as games leader. I organised all the activities on the camp. If it was raining I organised inside activities like face painting and arts and crafts. I had six children to look after. I settled them down at nights in their tents and I would read them stories before they went to sleep. Some of the children were very young; I looked after them like a mum would do. All the volunteers helped with the cooking duties, the washing up and the cleaning. We took the children on walks up to the caves and we took them swimming and at night we would sit round the campfire singing. It was a great experience and one that I would not have liked to have missed.

I loved working up at the Civic Centre with the office staff, we all worked together as a team: My manager Mrs Lynn Coupe, Miss Fiona Barnett, Mrs Helen Anderson, Sue and Mrs Joyce Bostock. It was a pleasure to have worked with all of them. Sheila had worked with David and myself while at Lochbuie, I used to sit with her up at the office and she would log me onto her computer to write a reply letter for her. She said I was good with words and that coming from Sheila was a bonus for me,

Sheila was one of the old school  when I first went to work for the Council.

Sue and Arch were helping the residents and giving 100% plus. We had all become good friends. I went on holiday for a week to Mablethorpe with Sue. What a week that was - we never stopped laughing! My friend Audrey was always there for me as well. She let us have her caravan at Sea Croft in Mablethorpe for a week. We shared the stories of our hilarious holiday with Lynn and Arch and they were pleased we had enjoyed our holiday. It was the start of a very good friendship. Jacky (my sister) and Graham told us that we were invited to Gavin and Louise's wedding to be held at Bestwood Park, Nottingham, on the 10th of October 1998. Gavin is a solicitor and they have two lovely sons, Harvey and Edward. Alan and Diane Meale are friends of Jacky and Graham's and were also guests at the wedding.

In March 1999 it was my 60th birthday. Jacky and Graham rang me to say they were taking me out for my birthday to Early Doors on Nottingham Road for a meal. Would I be ready and waiting for them to pick me up? On the way to the meal Graham asked if I minded waiting a minute while he called in at the Ukrainian Club, as he had promised to meet someone there. The club was opposite the Water Meadows swimming complex at the top of Bath Street. I followed Jacky and Graham into the club. It looked really dark, there was only a light on the bar. All of a sudden the lights came on. I couldn't believe my eyes. I recognised most of the people in there as I walked into the room to huge cheers. I was all dressed up but only had slippers on my feet - my feet were too swollen to get my shoes on. Jacky and Graham had said that nobody would notice because my feet would be under the table! I just stood there. For the first time in my life I was speechless. I didn't know if I should laugh or cry, so I just cried. All my family, my extended family, some of my very special friends, Barbara and Peter, Trevor and Pam, were there. Maureen and Micko set all the music up on the stage. My workmates and colleagues had all turned up for my birthday. Aunty Violet had brought my cousins, Jean and Janet. They had grown up living next door to us on Newgate Lane when we were children. Aunty Marian Crowder who had the coal yard and coal business on Bowling Street was there. So many turned up that I was just overwhelmed.

After that Jacky and Graham's youngest son, Paul, married Sam on the 9th of September 1999. They have two lovely children, Cameron and Esme. Paul and Sam are now approved foster carers for children with severe disabilities. They have a foster son, Callum, with autism. He never speaks and needs constant care. Jacky and her husband, Graham, are very proud parents and grandparents. They have just retired after working over

30 years in all weathers on the markets at Mansfield, Shirebrook and Sutton in Ashfield with their book stall. I am sure they will now be able to spend some precious time with their family.

While at Oakdene I went on holiday to the Dominican Republic with Pauline and another member of staff and members of the ladies darts and domino team from the Green Dragon. The holiday was spoilt because there was a fallout between our other member of staff and one of her friends that separated us all. None of us ever found out the truth, but things were not right. Pauline my colleague was totally snubbed, when she went back to work at the office, by the other member of staff who had been totally outcast by the group of friends we had gone on holiday with. This obviously made Pauline and myself very uncomfortable.

My daughter, Lynn, had left Sunnycroft in 2001. She told me she was going before she got pushed.  Lynn took another post at Kirkby Youth Housing, a charity run by a board of directors. It was for young people  from the age of 16 up to the age of 25.The staff used to help the young people to move on to independence with support. I was invited up to have a look round the hostel and was very impressed. They had a centre for the young people to learn skills, be creative, and for education. Judi Juno was the senior service manager and Lynn was the project worker managing the staff and young people. Judi and Lynn worked together and they became good friends. I was introduced to Judi and some of the board of directors and staff. Steve Wombwell worked with Lynn and was always a pleasure to talk to. It felt a privilege to be invited along to Judi's leaving night out. We all went to The Hutt on the Nottingham Road for a meal and a drink together. My cousin Sylvia's daughter, Carol, also worked at Kirkby Youth Housing for quite a long time. It was such a shame that Kirkby Youth closed down - it had helped so many young people.

My friends Arch and Sue used to invite me up for dinner on many occasions and Sue and I would play a game of darts after dinner. We were both in a darts team and the practice was good for us both. I would leave late in the evening to go home. One night as I was walking home I had crossed the road at the bottom of Park Avenue when a young lady approached me: she was very distressed. She asked if I was walking into Mansfield as she was frightened a man was following her. When we got to Crow Hill Drive I told her that was as far as I was going. She started to cry. "Please don't leave me," she said, "the man is still following me." I hadn't the heart to leave her so I invited her to come and have a cup of tea with me, with the promise that I would take her to her friends in town afterwards. She told me she was going to pick up a fix, as she was on cannabis and needed it to help her cope with her children. I told her if she loved her children she should give up the drugs or she would end up losing them. I walked with her into Mansfield and left her outside the night club on Clumber Street.

I made my way back home and went to bed at around 1.00am. Maureen from central control called, informing me that a lady was at the door asking for me. The young woman I had helped earlier was standing at the door. She was crying, "Please don't turn me away, I need your help." I took her up to my flat and put the kettle on to make her a coffee. She showed me a tin foil packet. Inside was a very small amount of cannabis that had cost her £10. It was taking all her money and she knew I had told her the truth that she would lose her children if she carried on taking the drugs. I would like to believe that if any of my children needed help someone would be there for them, so I sat up most of the night with this young mum. She asked me to go down to her home to meet her children. She lived on Sherwood Street, Mansfield Woodhouse. I went there after work the next day. She had two lovely children. I had a cup of tea with her and her husband. He wasn't on drugs. She showed me the foil with the cannabis still in the wrapper and promised me she would go for help to get off drugs.

At Stonecross we had a young man who was also on drugs. Janice was off duty and I was relieving her. A young girl of about 18 came screaming out of one of the flats saying her boyfriend had taken an overdose of drugs. Fortunately there was a workman from the Council on hand. I checked the young man. His pulse was rapid and he was unconscious. I asked the workman to stay with him while I ran to the office to make a 999 emergency call. The ambulance was very quick to respond and was at Stonecross in minutes. This young man put his own life at risk and could have died. Fortunately we acted quickly and he did recover.

At my own hostel one day I had just gone off duty and put my dinner on, when a resident came knocking on my flat door shouting for help. She said, "Mary, can you come quick, the baby in Flat 2 has swallowed something and she is going blue." I asked her to turn off the cooker and to use my phone to call an ambulance. I left her to do that while I was running out of the door to go down the stairs to Flat 2. The baby was on the floor struggling to breathe and was blue. I picked her up and put her over my knee upside down and slapped her back, until another resident said, "Mary, I've seen something come out of the baby's mouth - it's on the floor." It was a 1p coin. I lifted the baby back up and saw the colour coming back into her face. I was thinking, "Thank you, God". By the time the ambulance arrived the baby was sitting up and crawling like nothing had happened. I asked the ambulance to take the baby to hospital just to make sure that everything was okay. It was a good job I had done many years of First Aid training.

It was during 2001 that Lynn left, and Arch and Sue were dismissed: it was a great injustice. Everyone saw it coming but me. I was working up at Sunnycroft the day Arch and Sue had to hand in their keys and become homeless. This affected me badly as I felt that, in some way, I had let them down. They were standing on the grounds of Lochbuie crying and both were heartbroken. I had witnessed some very clever manipulation going on over a long period of time. While I was working up at Sunnycroft a warden started working in our office. She was supposed to be helping to start a crèche and we were asked to share our office with her. After only a short time she literally took over Arch's office, ignoring and undermining him. She also took over the phone, removing it from Arch's desk and putting it on her own. One day while Arch was off sick through stress and she was off duty, I was sent up to Sunnycroft to work. I accidently came across a large bundle of Arch's personal mail hidden in a drawer under books and paperwork. All this mail had been withheld from Arch and Sue. I did what I knew was the right thing: I went over to Lochbuie and posted the mail through Arch and Sue's letter box. The mistake I made was in failing to report it to the Council. I felt I had let Arch and Sue down.

After that another warden replaced Arch at Sunnycroft. I was sent up to help her with the bookwork. Both she and the crèche warden were in the office and whispering to each other all the time, ignoring me as if I wasn't there. Now I was being treated the same way Arch was. My life changed dramatically. Sue and Arch were the last to be fully trained co-ordinators. They were replaced by inexperienced people who I saw mess up our filing system and forget to give residents receipts, making it impossible to keep our records straight.

I was affected by all these errors that were made at a time when I was under my doctor and off work with stress. I went up to the Civic Centre to see the union rep and the personnel officer to tell them the truth of what happened to Arch and Sue and told them I feared I would be the next out. They told me that wouldn't happen. I was off sick for a long period of time but was fortunate to have a doctor who had known me for over three decades; he knew I was telling the truth. My mail was being withheld and some of my mail was opened and thrown on the floor in the hostel: a resident brought me up one of my payslips she had picked up off the floor. Only the two wardens I've referred to had a key to the post box. Another warden, Donna, was sent up to work at Stonecross. She didn't stay long: she brought the keys to my flat at Oakdene and left. She, also, was upset and under a lot of stress. I did try to return to work but I was ignored, belittled and disregarded. The stress I was working under was horrendous. I felt I couldn't trust anyone anymore. I was called up to the Civic to a meeting with the union rep and the personnel officer, with another member of staff. I was allowed to take my daughter Lynn with me for support. I was accused of making spurious remarks and of putting my residents at risk with my foster son. This was a total fabrication with no truth whatsoever.

My foster son, Paul, had lived with me and my family for over 12 years, and I knew he would never hurt anyone. Although part of my extended family I was told he wasn't allowed on the premises. Central control was told not to let him into my home. I lost my fight for justice: my spirit was broken. I had put up with continual bullying for over a year. It was a pivotal period of my life. In a distraught frame of mind I didn't think anyone believed me. I put my family through heartbreak because my mind was so restless and tormented. I know the truth and I know who pulled all the strings at the time. The injustice was never proved. The Council finally finished me on grounds of ill health in September2002, unaware of all the facts and the real situation.

This was the lowest point of my life. For 36 years I had campaigned for the homeless of Mansfield, seen the service develop to a very high standard, and been totally committed to working directly with many deprived and vulnerable individuals and families, helping to rescue their lives. This had brought me the appreciation and respect of the local caring agencies, and my work had been valued by the previous generation of councillors and council officers.

But those days were over and I had to move on, finding a way to cope with my frustration and anger over the injustice we had suffered. Were there any positives? Well, perhaps I should be grateful even, as it opened up a new phase of my life and new caring opportunities that I wouldn't have wanted to miss out on.

Thankfully Arch and Sue have also moved on with their lives. We are still good friends and keep in touch. It was sad that I had to end my career at the age of 62 trying to fight against a terrible injustice.

It is worth adding that Lochbuie, Sunnycroft and Oakdene - the heart of Mansfield's homelessness provision - were sold off soon after I left.

**Oakdene**

Canon Warburton used to visit me at Oakdene. He informed me that Oakdene was once his home. Originally the house belonged to St Peter's Church.

Stonecross was built in 1985 to house single young people and single parents with one child. It was to complete the hostel homeless housing provision specially built and supported by the Chief Executive of Mansfield

District Council, Geoff Lane. He had consulted both David and me about the accommodation we felt was the most needed at the time.

Mick and Mo, my friends, dressed as Santa and his helper

They were professional children's entertainers

# CHAPTER 13

# ADULT PLACEMENT & INDEPENDENT

# FOSTERING

After leaving Oakdene I was given a two-bedroomed house on Beck Crescent, Ladybrook Estate. That was in October 2002. I could not just sit down and do nothing. I soon made some friends on the Crescent, Ron and Marie ("Maz") Chillery, for example, who were already foster carers, so Marie and I had a lot in common. Hilda Collison was the first neighbour I met. It was Hilda who introduced me to Maz and Ron. The next door neighbours on my right were Mike and Janice Spencer who had two children, Gemma and James. We became very good friends and we used to go round to each other's houses. Sometimes I would help by having Gemma and James round at my house and the children would have meals with me. By December and coming up towards Christmas, I was beginning to get back to something like my old self. I also met up with Barbara, an old friend who had worked at the cinema with me when I was in my teens, so I was never short of friends dropping in. The next door neighbours on my left were Kay and her daughter, Naomi.

I contacted the Adult Placement Scheme to inform them I would like to give another young person a home; I had worked with them for the past 12 years. They placed a 17-year-old teenager with me, Chantelle. We got on well. She settled in okay and made herself at home. She told me that she wanted to be independent and have her own flat. That is what we agreed we would aim for. She met a young man and decided she wanted to be with him. I did tell her I didn't think she had known him long enough. She was only 17 but, like all teenagers, she wanted her freedom and I couldn't force her to stay. I did tell her she was welcome to keep in touch. I was working with Trish Murphy who was the Adult Placement Co-ordinator. She was very good and easy to work with. I went to the meetings and often met up with Trevor and Pam as well as other carers. Back in 1992 I had joined a course of 12 workshops arranged for staff working in residential homes for adults with severe learning disabilities. On this course I met a lovely lady, Ada Stewart, who had a daughter, Angela, with a learning disability. I met up with her again recently around at the shops on Ladybrook Square; it was nice to catch up with her news.

Trish sent Ricky to me, another 17-year-old who stayed with me for quite a long time. His problems were drug related. He was a very likeable lad, soft-hearted and caring of others. Although we worked on it together he hadn't the will power to give up the drugs. I will always remember Ricky, he was so like Steven who I had cared for at Oakdene and still came up to visit me and have a meal with us. Ricky moved on to live with some of his friends who had a house on Howard Road, off Westfield Lane.

Although I enjoyed working with people with learning disabilities I decided I wanted to get approved as a foster parent and care for children. I found I wasn't allowed to work for both schemes. Maz helped me to become a foster carer with Independent Fostering in Nottingham. John, who was staying with me temporarily at the time, was found a place in supported accommodation on York Street, Mansfield Woodhouse. Given a choice he would have loved to stay on with me. I was sorry to leave the Adult Placement Scheme but Trish understood me wanting to become a full time foster care. She sent me a lovely letter saying if I changed my mind I would always be welcome to go back to Adult Placement.

John Parr came to my home to explain all about "Independent Fostering". He and his wife, Margaret Kennedy, were the founders of the agency, which I joined and started to do my training with many others who were planning to become approved foster carers. I met some of the most genuine, caring people that I have ever worked with and some very dedicated social workers. John's wife, Margaret, always provided the food for our excellent meals. I would like to mention some of the friends who joined "Independent Fostering" at the same time as me: Rob and Bev Taylor, Jim and Kath Edwards, Alan and Jane Fletcher, Phil and Sue Simpson, Chris and Pam Love, Steve and Yvonne Shaw, and many more.

Then my Home Study started. Sarah Wells was the social worker who came to do my induction. I told her the truth, that I had gone through an injustice that had affected my health at the time. Since leaving the Council I had worked hard to regain my health. I gave her permission to go to the Council for a reference and agreed to a medical check, etc. In June 2003 I became an approved foster carer for teenagers and Sarah became my support social worker. We worked together well.

It was Margaret Kennedy who brought my first foster child from the agency on July 17, 2003. Sarah was a damaged child with special needs and presented the behaviour of a much younger child with learning difficulties. Sarah also showed slight signs of autism. I registered her at Queen Elizabeth's School on Chesterfield Road. She settled in and had no problems at first although she was behind in her schoolwork. She tried hard and I didn't put any pressure on her. She had been in five foster homes before she came to me and they had all given up on her. Sarah didn't trust anyone. She didn't want to go to bed at night - she used to sit on my stairs and cry for her mum, so I didn't get much sleep at first! Caroline Bull was Sarah's social worker and she was great. We worked together well and she supported both Sarah and myself. The agency supplied and paid for all the training that was important for the work. It covered many areas: the agency's policy and procedures, including relevant legislation and, in particular, the Children's Act, 1989, which had to be followed at all times. Then there were standards and regulations about safer caring, recording, food and hygiene, exploring values and discrimination, non-violent crisis intervention, preparation for independence, improving education and positive outcomes, and much more! John Parr advised me to get a computer and learn how to use it for running records, emailing and research. He also advised me to go to college to get my NVQ qualification in Caring for Young People and Children. So in January 2004, at the age of 65, I went to Basford College near Nottingham to study. One of my tutors was Tina, and Christine was my assessor. They were amazed at my experience and knowledge. It was while I was at college that the Children's Act was updated and we studied the "five outcomes" and that "every child mattered". It was a two year course that I successfully completed in seven months. The agency paid my college fees for me.

I would not have been able to achieve any of this without the support I got from John and Margaret and the other carers. It proved to me that we are never too old to learn. I decided to do some voluntary work for Framework (a homelessness charity) at the same time. I used to go down to the Framework Centre on Sherwood Street to help Sue with the breakfasts and lunches, cleaning and serving the meals and making cups of tea. I also did a sponsored swim of 20 lengths of the pool at Sherwood Baths to raise funds for Framework.

Around this time I had written quite a few poems and completed my first poetry book, which was edited and printed by Pro Print at Peterborough. I paid for the books to be printed and sold them to friends, family and carers, again to raise funds for Framework. I handed the cheque to the manager of the centre on Sherwood Street, Mansfield. Framework were doing so much for the homeless people of Mansfield and Ashfield: they were serving meals, letting the homeless have showers, supplying them with food, clothing, toiletries, bedding, and sleeping bags for those who were sleeping rough and in tents. The staff were also helping them with benefits and finding them homes and accommodation. All the homeless, including mothers and children, were being given assistance. My friend, Jenny, who worked for Framework at that time, went with me to count the lengths as I swam them.  As you can tell my heart was still with the homeless people of our town.

In 2006 Sarah's teacher left the school and Sarah became the victim of bullying. She would go to school and get angry, running round slamming doors, putting herself and others in danger and we had to protect her. Sarah had become a loner with no friends and she was with other children who had problems very similar to her own. I had already taught Sarah boundaries and routines by using a star chart and rewarding rather than punishing. Sarah felt safe at home - I had promised her I would never give up on her. Sarah's school was wanting to exclude her permanently as they found it difficult to deal with. Whenever Sarah got excluded I used to sit and help her with maths and other subjects. She also had a teacher who used come to our home, as her exclusions would sometimes last for a full week.

It was decided we would give Sarah extra support to try and keep her in education and a team of us, which included Mr Savage, Sarah's tutor, Tony Stevens and Sue Denham, education officers, Eli Buffer from CAMHS and our supporting social workers all attended regular monthly meetings at the school. Sarah was sent to the learning intervention centre with Sharon Clay - the one teacher Sarah trusted and confided in. She had worked with Sarah throughout her time at Queen Elizabeth School and understood her needs. We worked together successfully and Sarah stayed in education up until she left school in 2008. She then went on to West Notts College to continue with her education.

My time with Independent Fostering made me realise all the work John and Margaret put into the agency and all the responsibilities they had undertaken. They laid on parties, took us to the panto at the Theatre Royal, and gave all the carers a day out at a spa where I taught Irene, one of the carers, to swim. However, they decided it was time for them to move on and Independent Fostering was merged with Fostering People in 2007. We were transferred to the new agency. I went to John and Margaret's leaving party and hoped they had made the right decision. I really felt that the experience I'd gained with Independent Fostering was priceless and that I had done the right thing in returning to caring.

# CHAPTER 14

# FOSTERING PEOPLE

Joining Fostering People was another bonus. Although I had experience and knowledge, I realised there was still a lot to learn and I attended all the training on offer. Some of our supporting social workers transferred over to Fostering People with us: I still had Sharon as my support worker.

Sarah was in her last year at school. I met a lot of new carers from Mansfield and surrounding areas. We used to go to the Nottingham support group meeting at the Old Spot pub at Daybook. Sharon, Rob and I thought it would be a good idea to set up a new local support group nearer to Mansfield. We found our venue - the Staff of Life in Sutton. The monthly meetings meant carers could get together to support each other and to share experiences. The agency financed the venue and paid for all the carers' meals. Sharon always attended our meetings. Our support group soon began to grow. The manager and founder, Sarah Byatt, organised a trip to the American Adventure Park for all the carers and the children to meet up together for a day out. She stood at the entrance to the park with the social workers giving us all our tickets. The rain poured down most of the day and we were all buying waterproof coats, though the weather dried up later. My foster daughter, Sarah, and I sat chatting to one of our social workers, Janet Litowczuk and her two sons, so we must have been among the last to leave.

Another fun event ("It's a Knock Out!") celebrating the 10th anniversary of Fostering People was held at the Harvey Haddon stadium, Nottingham. Carers were invited to bring their own children along with foster children. I took my grandchildren, Chance and Aaliyah, who joined in all the fun along with my daughter, Lynn. We took a packed lunch and had a picnic on the grass. Before leaving the stadium, when the awards were being handed out our manager, Sarah, mentioned that she would be leaving the agency so that she could spend more time at home with her family. It had been a pleasure working with her. Every year the agency provided days out and special events. John Platt, our new manager, social workers, and staff joined us at Drayton Manor Park - finding the time to share the day with all the foster carers and children. The agency was still expanding and employing more new carers who then joined our support group; we were all working together.

In 2009 Sharon told me that carers were going to be asked to work towards a new qualification - the CWDC

(Children Workforce Development Council). This was a vision to build a world class workforce for children, young people and families, involving everyone in the field of caring working together at a professional level. We were given a book to complete eight activities under the Children's Acts: 1. The United Nations convention on the rights of children - understanding the principles and values essential for foster caring; 2. Family and social relationships; 3. Effective recording; 4. The Children's Acts, 1989 parental responsibility; 5. Safeguarding and child protection - Section 47 of The Children's Act; 6. The National Assessment Framework - promoting children's and young peoples' needs; 7. The Children's Act 2004; and 8. Core standards skills and competences for foster carers. With all the training and a lot of hard work and determination, I completed my CWDC portfolio on the 26th February, 2010, at the age of 71.

Looking at this framework - as a foster carer and from my own perspective - I realised that it covered what I had automatically been doing on a day-to-day basis throughout my working life. I have continually updated my knowledge and my skills by attending training and working as a part of a team with all the professional bodies wherever possible. I updated my knowledge of policies and procedures and I have always adhered to the legislation and been eager to research, study and improve my knowledge. It is very important to put into practice all the skills required by the National Assessment Framework. I have worked with many professional people to safeguard and promote the well-being of children, young people and children with disabilities. It is every child's right to have a caring, loving home with the security, stability, warmth, safety and all the benefits that all children gain when they are cared for and loved.

Sharon had been my support social worker for over four years and her support to both Sarah and me proved just how dedicated she was to her work. We were sorry to see her leave. And Sarah's social worker for many years, Caroline Bull, left just after Sharon. Both these social workers were outstanding. Sarah's new social worker was Karen Cann. At Sarah's last review before leaving school, all the members of our team who had worked together to keep her in education turned up, including Geoff Vincent from West Notts College. He was going to be Sarah's support at the college when Sarah moved on. In 2008, Sue Denham, the education officer, worked with Geoff and continued to support Sarah after care. Meeting people like this makes me feel very privileged. It has given me the strength and determination to continue through my life's journey and vocation.

John Platt, our Fostering People manager, used to invite all the carers to the East Midlands Foster Carers' Forum which was held every three months to update all the carers, social workers and staff on upcoming activities, carers' awards, children's achievements, the progress of the agency, Ofsted reports etc. I enjoyed attending the forums and was fortunate to have Ian Wilkinson, one of our local carers, give me a lift to all of the agency's meetings and support group events. I met my new support social worker, Jackie Dicks, at one of the forums. She also attended all our carers' meetings. On one occasion we all turned up at our Sutton venue only to discover that the room had been double-booked and a wedding party was already seated: there was no room at the inn. I told Jackie I knew a venue that would probably be able to help - The Star at Woodhouse where Janice, one of my residents at Beech Avenue in the 70s, was the landlady. I couldn't contact Janice by phone so 16 of us arrived unannounced. Janice being Janice she just took it in her stride, quickly getting her top room ready and serving us all with our meals, desserts and drinks. All the carers were happy with both the food and service. The Star became our regular venue from then until Janice took over The Bull on Woodhouse Road and we followed her there.

Jackie, my support social worker, left and moved away from Nottingham to be near to her children. We had got on well together. My new social worker was Andi Lilley-Tams. The carers' Christmas dinner was held at The Bull. The room was full, everyone had turned up and our manager, John, joined us for the meal. This proves how much respect the agency has for all their staff and carers.

Sarah was doing well at West Notts College for two years until 2010. Unfortunately, she was then transferred to a different teaching base in Sutton-in- Ashfield. Because of her autism she couldn't cope with the change. Sarah had chosen to stay on with me after she reached 18 and was no longer in the care of the Local Authority. Sarah somehow had slipped through the net. Since Sarah first came to me it was always acknowledged at meetings and reviews that she was a young person with special needs. Sarah was given a new social worker who only attended two of her reviews and came to the first review without any knowledge of her background. The reviewing officer had been supporting Sarah and had all her review reports. It was agreed that she would still need support after leaving school, but Sarah's social worker from the Social Services Department said that she was "only a puppet" and that she would get no support from Social Services unless she moved out and into her own accommodation at the age of 18. Suddenly Social Services had decided that Sarah was no longer a person with special needs!

I contacted a solicitor to fight for Sarah's rights. The solicitor got a six month payment to support Sarah for the period after she left school in 2008. Not only did Sarah's support end, she failed to receive any leaving-care grants. Since leaving care her benefits have not covered her needs. I have had to support Sarah out of my own income to buy her shoes, clothing and personal needs items for the past six years. I have taught her how to budget and recognise what her priorities are. Sarah will be 24 in February, 2016. I want her to be able to cope with her life if anything happens to me. The Fostering People agency still supports Sarah today if she needs help towards finding employment. Sarah has worked at Kings Mill Hospital in the voluntary service. She has had several interviews for work but unfortunately not been successful. Sarah goes on looking for employment and is very good on a computer and with technology generally.

In August 2010 I lost Fred, the brother we had searched for and found during my time at Sunnycroft. My niece, Janet, my sister-in-law, Dorothy, and I used to visit him in hospital when he was really poorly with his illness. Dorothy and Janet took him back home to look after him with the help of carers and nurses. We had spent over 35 years being a complete family together and sharing our lives at every opportunity. We will always have fond memories of a very special brother. Our families will always stay close and will always be there for each other.

In 2011 I was given another 16-year-old foster child who hadn't been able to settle down in her previous placement. She stayed with me for a year. I took her on holiday to Skegness and Blackpool, allowed her friends into my home and included them in the holidays so that she would have company of her own age. Nevertheless, she missed her family and desperately wanted to go back home. I was going with her to CAMHS - a mental health service that helps young children and adolescents on St John Street - almost every two weeks. I was going up to her school to support her. The placement didn't work out and she moved on to another family. I wish her all the best and hope that she learnt something from the time she spent with me. I also did some respite care for Sue and Phil Simpson, looking after a little girl, Kerry, while they had a break from caring for her. They knew that Kerry enjoyed staying with me. She was a lovely, happy girl who loved music, singing and dancing. I also took her to Skegness while I was her respite care and I loved having Kerry and I know that she enjoyed her time with me.

My brother, Frank, called to see me and asked if Sarah and I wanted to spend five days in Blackpool with him and his wife Sandra. I had not seen Frank for a long time. I agreed to go, hoping we could have some time together. Despite past events, I had always forgiven him and I do feel for him. While we were on holiday he was suffering with vertigo and I was worried about him. He has not been in very good health since we got back from the holiday. I keep in contact with him over the phone - I just like to make sure he is alright. My heart always rules my head!

During the last two years I have been helping some of the carers with their CWDC qualification - there is a lot they have to learn. I was given another placement in August 2012, a young woman called Tash. Her social worker was Sarah Patterson who had been Sarah's school teacher when she was at Queen Elizabeth's School. Tash reminded me of myself when I was young. I took to her despite the fact that she had a temper and didn't like rules and routines. One evening she came in angry at the world because of something that had happened while she was out with her friends. They must have really upset her. I knew she wasn't angry with me but she wanted to shout at someone. I told her that I understood how she was feeling but asked her to go up to her room to calm down - I would be in the conservatory when she felt she could come and talk to me. After a while Tash came and apologised for shouting at me. We then began to have respect for each other. She told me she didn't like the fact that she was almost 17 and wasn't allowed to have a stay-over with her friends or stay out later at a friend's party. It was an issue I promised to take up with both social workers, but she'd have to be patient until her review.

Tash was now over 17 and could have left at any time. She didn't want to leave, she just wanted to be trusted and have some private time like all teenagers. I really enjoyed the challenge. Tash found it hard to accept authority of any kind and tended to let people think she didn't care about anybody or anything. I wanted to prove to her that she was worth something. More than that, I wanted to find the real Tash, the other side of her that she didn't want people to see. She had put up a barrier to protect herself from being hurt. All she wanted was to be listened to and for people to accept her as she was. I was prepared to listen, and I was prepared to wait for Tash to trust me. The review was attended by Kayley Spinks who had taken over as my new supporting social worker while Andi was on maternity leave. As you can see, social workers are always coming and going and it isn't always easy - for us or the new social workers - when we all have to make a new start: we have to rebuild a new working relationship. I have been very fortunate in being able to adjust to the new situations and seem to have a natural gift for making people feel comfortable and at ease in my company. I arranged a meeting knowing that Tash's review was coming up with both our social workers so that she could discuss her concerns and feelings and to know the best way of sorting out her problems. This is what I mean by team work: to know where we all stand and how to act together in the best interests of a child or young person.

We put forward the issues at the review. Steve was a new reviewing officer. During the review Tash went outside and let my little dog, Petra, into the sitting room. Petra jumped on to Steve's knee and, in her excitement, did a wee all over Steve's paperwork and trousers. I just stood there apologising for my dog. The other social workers struggled to keep a straight face. I went to find Tash. She had gone to Sarah's room and both Tash and Sarah were laughing hysterically over Steve's misfortune. I had to bring Tash back into the review and I could see she was struggling to keep her face straight. I had fetched a clean cloth for Steve to wipe his paperwork and to wipe his trousers dry. I did feel bad about the incident. After this episode it was agreed by all that Tash needed support and a base. The next time I saw Steve he told me the incident had made a lot of his colleagues laugh - and that he could now see the funny side. The plan was that Tash had to prove to me that she was safe by informing me where she was and where she was staying, keeping in touch with me on her mobile and giving me a telephone contact. Tash agreed and most of the time her contact was her sister, Leanne, who she brought home to meet me. Leanne and I agreed that we would work together to support Tash.

Somehow things seemed to sort themselves out, though we did have blips now and again. We saw an amazing improvement in Tash: she turned her life around in a very short time. Both Sarah and I were invited to Leanne's home to the christening of two of her children and to the christening party, where I met Tash's mum and dad and other members of her family. Leanne's partner, James, also became friends with me and I love their children. I also had the pleasure of meeting James' mum, Catherine. They are a lovely family. I took Tash on holiday to Greece with my family. Tash was absolutely great with my great grandchildren, teaching them to swim. The holiday was brilliant and it gave Tash a chance to get to know my family. I also took her with me to spend a holiday in Skegness with my sister-in-law, Barbara. I had never seen Tash so relaxed. We went out every day and had a lot of fun. We spent what I call some "prime time" together. It does make me feel proud to be able to get along with young people considering my age!

Tash was 18 in September 2013 and leaving care. I made the decision to retire at the age of 74. Tash was my last foster child. She had met her boyfriend, James, and they were planning to move into a house together when she left care on her 18th birthday. They set up a home on the same street as her sister so that Leanne could give them support. I bought Tash and James some presents to help towards their home, plus a coffee table. Unfortunately the relationship broke down. Tash has since moved into another relationship that she is happy in and I have met her new partner, Sandy Nelson. Tash will always be welcome to visit me and my family anytime.

Sarah was my first foster placement in 2003. She has stayed on with me since leaving the care system in 2008 and is a part of my extended family. The agency gave me a retirement party at The Bull, Woodhouse Road. They did me proud: I was overwhelmed. The party was attended by John, my manager, Jill, the service manager, and Sarah Wells who had supported me throughout my 10 years of fostering. Sarah Harding from the agency made me a beautiful retirement cake. Although Andi was not back from maternity leave she made a surprise visit to be there for me. Lots of other people came: my daughter and granddaughter, my foster children, Sarah, Tasha and her partner James, Trevor and Pam Lewis, Audrey Cook, Rob and Bev Taylor, Margaret from the Nottingham group, and all the carers from the Mansfield support group. Janice, the landlady, and her staff worked hard on the catering. I felt that everyone did me proud. I was presented with my 10 years service certificate, a Fostering People pen, and a 10 year glass trophy, as well as lots of cards, presents and flowers.

After the past 10 years of working with all concerned I have no doubt that being a foster carer is a very worthwhile career and that it takes special, dedicated, committed people who love children and young people to accept them into their homes and make them a part of their families and their lives. They are an invaluable asset to our country.

Since my retirement from fostering I have joined Jigsaw, a registered charity which supports people over the age of 60 in the Mansfield/Ashfield area who live alone with little or no family contact. They offer housing-related support, an independence service, and a befriending service. I became a befriender for Kath and love visiting her. We get included in social outings such as a river cruise on the Trent, organised by Cate Bones, the befriending co-ordinator. Other volunteers and the people on the trip were friendly, helpful, and a pleasure to talk to. Being a volunteer makes you realise just how much of a difference you can make to someone's life.

Although I am now retired I want to go on helping in the community. I go into the charity shop on the Ladybrook Square and have made some very special friends. The people of the Ladybrook Estate are a close and friendly community. All the shops on the square join forces with residents of the estate and put on a Christmas fair. All donations go to charity. It makes a fun day out for all concerned and is usually held a week before Christmas.

I enjoy listening to Radio Nottingham as I don't watch a lot of television these days. I find it far more interesting to hear other listeners sharing their personal views, stories and life experiences. The East Midlands, Nottingham, Lincoln, Leicestershire, and Derbyshire have all become like a radio family. Amanda Bowman was the first presenter to give me the confidence to speak on the radio. Now I am listening and joining in with Verity Cowley, Frances Finn, Dean Jackson, and Paul Robey. I don't like to miss Paul's show on Sundays from 12 lunch till 4.00pm. He plays music from the 50s, 60s and 70s. Then there's the lovely Radio Caroline online, taking all the calls. I have also had the pleasure of meeting Michaela who came to record my wartime stories for our Victory in Europe day. I have saved the recording for my family. I do miss the Late Show and Jenny and all the late night callers. I have met up with Vee in Mansfield and I hope one day to meet magical Mary from Arnold. I continue to write short stories and new poems. Over the past two years I have written poetry for the Byron Society - for Ken Purslow, the chairman and secretary from Hucknall. Ken has entered two of my poems into the Maureen Crisp Memorial poetry competition and I have been the runner up both times.

I feel that I have led a very extraordinary life. Now at the age of 76 I can say I don't have any regrets about working in the caring profession for over 47 years, working with people aged from the cradle to the grave. Above all, my life has been dedicated to the plight of the homeless, but it has also included young people from broken homes, foster children and many others.

My own children always had to share me while they were growing up so I am proud that they have grown up into adults who are also hard-working, caring, loving parents, grandparents, and role models. I have something valuable that money can't buy: a close and loving extended family and some very special friends. Sarah is still with me at the age of 24 and is not planning to move on until she feels she is ready.

My daughter Lynn got remarried in June 2014 to Mark Smith, better known to the family as Smitty. In the same month 29 members of our family spent a whole week together in Greece for her 50th birthday and went to the church in Kassiopi, where they had their wedding blessed. For me it was amazing. My son, Paul, and his family came to Kassiopi from Germany with my grandchildren, Jacqueline and Dominic. We all stayed in the same apartments. It was a shame that 3 grandchildren – Aaliyah, Chance and Essence - couldn't be there due to school exams.

What my book demonstrates is that all the people of Mansfield, Ashfield and Nottingham can be proud that people from all walks of life and professions have given so much back to our society, with a lot of compassion and dedication.

**All my family in Greece**

**My children, grandchildren and great grandchildren at my daughter's wedding**

# Proud to be Mansfield born and bred

*I'm a Mansfield girl born and bred*
*It's a great little town it must be said*
*Interesting history, dating back; this I know:*
*There is no other place I'd wish to go*

*Sherwood Forest and its legends of Robin Hood*
*The Sheriff of Nottingham always after his blood*
*Lord Byron lived local on Quarry Lane*
*He became a poet that rose to fame*

*Newstead Abbey in its beautiful surround*
*The White Lady that walks the lake, that drowned*
*Mines, mills and factories long since gone*
*People of the town still standing strong*

*We fight to keep our little town alive*
*Accepting the changes, learnt us how to survive*
*The place I'll always be proud to lay my head*
*Is Mansfield town where I was born and bred.*

# ACKNOWLEDGEMENTS

I would like to thank Trevor Lewis for working with me on my autobiography, patiently improving the punctuation and layout. Thank you, Trevor, and thank you Pam, Trevor's wife, for giving me the confidence to write my book.

I would also like to thank Sarah, my foster daughter, for assisting me throughout and using her computer skills as my secretary. Thank you Sarah, I love you!

Thank you to all the people who have given me their consent to include their names. Thank you to everyone that helped me fight for the plight of the homeless. Thank you to all the people I have had the pleasure of working with, who have given me the support to enable me to change the lives of many vulnerable people in our society.

Thank you to John Platt, our manager at Fostering People, who has expanded the agency into a successful company covering several counties, Wales and Scotland, achieving an "outstanding" rating from Ofsted.

Thank you to Roundwood Surgery and all the GPs, nurses, and staff who have supported me, my family and all my residents for over 40 years.

Thank you to all my family for supporting me and accepting into our extended family the many people who have shared our lives.

And, lastly, a thank you to my sister, Jacky, and her husband, Graham, for being there for me throughout my life, and giving me their help and advice while I have been writing this autobiography.

# HISTORY OF MY FAMILY

# BACKGROUND

# MY DAD'S FAMILY

My dad's family has been well known in Mansfield for over six generations, dating back to before 1772. My great-great grandfather was born on Duck Lane on March 31st, 1842. He married Harriet Allen on December 25th, 1861. He was a coal man. They lived on Foundry Yard, off Clumber Street, which is now the Wilko's car park. They had 12 children and lost two. Ten children survived and they were all involved in the coal industry. The first mine sunk in the Mansfield area was Sherwood pit followed by Crown Farm. My grandfather was George Crowder. He married Sarah Anne Fell. They had seven children and were coal merchants who lived at 64 Newgate Lane. My dad, Frank, started his own coal business before I was born. When I was growing up my dad and his brother, my uncle Cyril, both became coal merchants, still on Newgate Lane. Their garage was across the road from Winston's chemist. My dad's uncle, William, known as Bill Crowder had his coal business at 15a Bowling Street. He ran it with his sons, Walter and Harry. Walter Crowder married Marion Birkhamshaw and they had two children, Walter and Gillian. Two of my dad's cousins, Thomas Crowder and Samuel Crowder, started up their own business in the fruit and vegetable trade. They worked in and around Mansfield and stood on Mansfield market for many years. That business was passed down to their grandson, Ray Crowder, and his wife, Patricia, who lived at Woodhouse on Brown Avenue. My sister, Jacqueline, and her husband, Graham, have just retired after over 30 years of standing on the market with their book stalls in Mansfield, Shirebrook and Sutton. They were well known to many people. The only remaining coal business is on Bowling Street and Colin Crowder could be the last coal merchant in the history of our generation. All the coal mines have closed down, Thorseby being the last. Our coal industry in Mansfield and throughout the whole of Nottinghamshire has gone forever.

Grandma Crowder and Aunty May

(My dad's mother and sister in 1910)

# HISTORY OF MY FAMILY

# BACKGROUND

# MY MUM'S FAMILY

My mum's family tree can be traced back to Robert Lamb, born 1644, who married Joan Chadwick and lived at Oxton, near Southwell. The family later moved to Burton Joyce. My great grandad, Thomas Lamb, was born there in 1849. In 1874 he married Elizabeth Ann Saxon who was born in 1851, and they moved to the Bleakhills in Mansfield. They had eight children. My grandmother, Christian Saxon Lamb, was born at the Bleakhills in 1883 and married James William Mason in 1907. The Saxton family run a grocery shop at 8 Clumber Street, Mansfield and my grandmother worked there until she got married. My grandparents had six children. My mother was Gertrude Mason, born in 1912. She married my father, Frank Crowder, in 1936. My mum's first child was stillborn. She also lost my youngest brother, George, at the age of six months to meningitis. My family are still researching the family tree, but it has become clear that both sides have long had connections with Mansfield, Sutton and Nottinghamshire.

Granddad and Grandma Mason, my mum's parents, in

1907